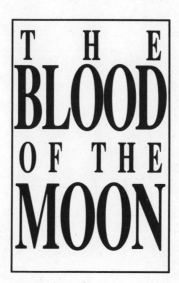

THE
BLOOD
OF THE
MOON

THE BLOOD OF THE MOON

The Roots Of The Middle East Crisis

GEORGE GRANT

Wolgemuth & Hyatt, Publishers, Inc.
Brentwood, Tennessee

The mission of Wolgemuth & Hyatt, Publishers, Inc. is to publish and distribute books that lead individuals toward:

- A personal faith in the one true God: Father, Son, and Holy Spirit;

- A lifestyle of practical discipleship; and

- A worldview that is consistent with the historic, Christian faith.

Moreover, the Company endeavors to accomplish this mission at a reasonable profit and in a manner which glorifies God and serves His Kingdom.

Unless otherwise noted, all Scripture quotations are from the author's own translation.

All Scripture quotations marked NKJV are from the New King James Version of the Bible, © 1979, 1980, 1982, 1984 by Thomas Nelson, Inc., Nashville, Tennessee and are used by permission.

Koranic quotations are from *The Koran: A Modern English Reader,* © 1977, 1981 by Khalid Al Mansour Publisher, London and are used by permission.

Wolgemuth & Hyatt, Publishers, Inc.
1749 Mallory Lane, Suite 110
Brentwood, Tennessee 37027

ISBN 1-56121-076-5

To David Dunham and Bill Breslin
Who Hold Me Accountable

To Karen, Joel, Joanna, and Jesse
Who Simply Hold Me

And

To the Courageous Participants
In Operation Desert Storm
Who Hold Us All

Joyeuse Garde

CONTENTS

Part Three: The Future and Faith

FOREWORD

What is the goal of Saddam Hussein? For an answer to this question, *The Blood of the Moon* is a must reading. This book points out that the current struggle in the Middle East is but a continuation of the ongoing enmity between Arab and Jew. The resulting contention when Abraham fathered a son, Ishamael, by the concubine Hagar and later fathered another son, Isaac, born of his wife, Sarah, is still a burden the world bears today.

The Blood of the Moon asks whether American involvement in the desert sands, part of an acclaimed effort on behalf of the United Nations for a "new world order," is a modern day Tower of Babel, the Crusades revisited, or the ghost of Napoleon Bonaparte who sought to achieve French hegemony in the region.

Or is Saddam Hussein simply striving to restore the grandeur of Babylon under Nebuchadnezzar, or trying to be a conqueror like Suleiman or Saladin?

The world did not want to believe Hitler's rhetoric as stated in *Mien Kampf*. Sadaam Hussein has stated clearly that he wants *"Ji'had,"* a holy war against non-Moslems. Will we believe him?

The ultimate question of judgment for America is whether the potential for Iraq's development of nuclear, chemical, and biological weapons coupled with the prospect for world terrorism justifies our investment of blood and treasure which armed conflict will produce? Does Iraq's threat to engulf the world in a *Ji'had* justify U.S. involvement?

All Americans interested in events of the Middle East, especially Jews, Christians, and Moslems, will be richly rewarded by reading this sobering, referenced analysis of what may become America's entrance into the most volatile region of our planet.

Congressman WILLIAM E. DANNEMEYER

ACKNOWLEDGEMENTS

H enry David Thoreau once remarked, "The scholar rarely writes as well as the farmer talks." As I have undertaken the task of writing this book, the truth of that observation has struck me anew. The many ordinary and extraordinary people that have contributed to my thinking—Thoreau's farmers and their modern kith and kin—may very well have been able to articulate the roots of the crisis in the Middle East better than I could have. In any case, it is clear enough to me that without their many kindnesses this book would not have been possible.

Two of America's most incisive experts in Middle Eastern affairs, General Richard Secord and General Daniel Graham, took time out from their very hectic schedules to brief me on the geo-political situation in the region as well as the basis for United States military and diplomatic policy. Similarly, Joel Belz and Martin LaBeuf—visionary publishers of *World Magazine* and *The Middle East Business Report*, respectively—shared with me their informed insights and perspectives.

A number of Christian Arabs from Syria, Lebanon, Iraq, Egypt, Jordan, and Algeria helped me focus my research and hone my arguments. The lives and testimonies of Philip Hamid, Georges Corm, Rabit Shehadeh, Johan Neguib, Rachid Shahhat, and Laila Abou Saif remain a marvel to me.

Several Syrian, Iranian, and Iraqi exiles shared with me not only their opinions and experiences, but also their warm hospitality and abiding friendship. I am particularly grateful for the time and effort that Nayef al Barras,

Ibraham Abu Ayyad, Muhammad Kamel, Sakib Aziz, and Arslan Qutb have invested in this project.

In Israel, my friends Offer Eshed, Dafna Furst, Reba Cohen, and Michael Miamon made my time in their strife-riven nation both fruitful and enjoyable. Several members of the Knesset were also very helpful in providing data and insights generally unavailable to American journalists and in sharing openly both their hopes and their fears for the generations to come. My special thanks go to Uzi Landau, Tzachi Hanegbi, and Elyakim Haetzni. In addition, General Joshua Sagi, former assistant director of Israeli Military Intelligence, was very generous with his time and personal perspective of the regional conflict.

Rana Ardaji, Dr. Wahib Dajani, Khalil Touma, and Nehaya al Helo, all leaders in the Palestinian *Intifada,* graciously briefed me on the problems faced by Arabs in the Judean and Samarian sectors of the West Bank. In addition, the editorial staff of *Al Fajr,* a Palestinian newspaper produced in Jerusalem, were very helpful and provided me with transcriptions and translations of hard-to-find Arabic documents, stories, and interviews that I could not possibly have obtained on my own.

James B. Jordan and Michael Hyatt helped me sort through all the tangled theological issues that could very easily have stymied this project. Jim's insight on the connection between the Tower of Babel and the New Word Order, and Mike's insight into the plight of Arab Christians proved to be invaluable. I am grateful for their wisdom and their friendship.

My staff back in the United States served selflessly in thankless tasks all during the researching and writing of this book. Jim Small accompanied me to the Middle East taking care of security, itinerary, and a hundred other incidentals. Mark Horne worked long hours tracking down obscure details and collecting necessary bibliographic resources. Bill Breslin, Alan Harkey, Ed Mahoney, Gail Brown, Carol Sue Quarquesso, Susan Allen, Jennifer Burkett, Kathy Israels, Bill Sidebottom, and Bob Allen supported this project with their encouragement, their ideas, their hard work, and their prayers. And, of course, Mary Jane Morris held down the fort.

As always, my family has been tremendously supportive. They have withstood my many absences with grace, and they have shared fully in my calling and my vision. Any success this project may ever inure must surely be theirs.

Theodore Roosevelt, a man who was amazingly prolific and phenomenally successful throughout his life, once said:

> No other success in life—not being President, or being wealthy, or going to college, or writing a book, or anything else—comes up to the success of the man and woman who can feel that they have done their duty and that their children and grandchildren rise up to call them blessed.[1]

Recognizing that, it is my prayer that what I *do* before the watching eyes of my family never supersedes what I *am*.

Third Week of Advent
Jerusalem

INTRODUCTION

Time after time mankind is driven against the rocks of the horrid reality of a fallen creation. And time after time mankind must learn the hard lessons of history—the lessons that for some dangerous and awful reason we can't seem to keep in our collective memory.

Hilaire Beloc

You cannot escape the revelation of the identical by taking refuge in the illusion of the multiple.

G. K. Chesterton

When wars and rumors of wars grab the full attentions of men and women the world over—wrenching us from our daily routines, our families, and our ongoing responsibilities—one question looms large: Why? Why is this happening?

No single book can hope to answer that question fully. Indeed, as the great Victorian preacher, Charles Haddon Spurgeon has said:

I would have everybody able to read, and write, and cipher; indeed I don't think a man can know too much; but mark you, the knowing of these things is not education; and there are millions of your reading and writing people who are as ignorant as neighbor Norton's calf, that did not know its own mother.[1]

Even so, I am convinced that a partial answer to that question can be discerned. And this book is simply an attempt to accomplish just that.

1

ð«   ð«   ð«

The structure of this brief study is fairly straightforward:

Chapter 1 is an overview of the current dilemmas that we face in the Middle East—and their dramatic historical import.

In chapter 2, the human dimension of the current conflict in the Middle East is told through a series of vignettes and the personal reflections of the people most affected by it.

Chapter 3 provides a cursory review of the history of the great empires of the East—Egypt, Persia, Assyria, and Babylon—and how the ideas of those ancient pagan civilizations actually continue to shape modern Islamic aspirations.

Chapter 4 recounts the primordial enmity between the rival children of Abraham: between Ishmael, son of Haggar, and Isaac, son of Sarah; between Moslem and Jew; between the Arabs and Israel.

Chapter 5 details an extension of that same rivalry in the struggle between Islam and Christianity, beginning with the territorial disputes between Byzantium and the early caliphs and continuing through the Crusades on up to the present.

Chapter 6 examines the attempts of the West to resolve the grave dilemmas of the area, focusing particularly on the efforts of the British, French, and Russians following World War I and the breakup of the Ottoman Empire.

Chapter 7 is a Biblical look at the whole idea of a New World Order, beginning with the Tower of Babel and extending to the United Nations and the Bush administration.

Chapter 8 is an examination of American foreign policy, the worldviews that shape it, and the possibility of that policy forging a lasting peace in the Middle East.

Finally, chapter 9 concludes this brief study with a personal vignette and reflection.

A bibliography is included for further reading, though it is far from complete. Only those books actually consulted for this book are included.

A note on the epigrams that open each chapter and each section may be prudent at this point. None of the passages of Scripture or quotations from various Islamic texts are used as mere window dressing. In fact, they are an integral part of the sociological and philosophical hermeneutic that the book attempts to both expound and exemplify. My work is self-consciously Western and epistimologically Christian—hopefully without the taint of syncretism or heterodoxy. Certainly, the old adage is true, "There is no such thing as presuppositionless exegesis." Thus, the epigrams are not added for mere aesthetic appearances but for their value in demonstrating the vast worldview gulf between East and West as well as for their vivid portrayal of the continuing relevance of the Bible's innumerable prophetic passages—a continuing relevance that extends even beyond their immediate or primary fulfillments.

🙡 🙡 🙡

Although my academic background is in Middle Eastern politics, this is the first book that I have had the opportunity to devote entirely to that subject. The temptation to make it a tediously footnoted treatise was therefore quite strong. I resisted that temptation for the sake of both timeliness and accessibility. I wanted as many people as possible to have access to the information as soon as possible, so I rapidly put the manuscript together. I am probably more aware than anyone of the limitations that a book like this inevitably has. I have opted purposefully for a cursory look at the issues, thus, the unashamedly slender volume you now hold.

Charles Haddon Spurgeon excused the brevity of one of his books by jesting:

> If this were a regular sermon preached from a pulpit, of course, I should make it long and dismal, like a winter's night, for fear people should call me eccentric. As it is

only meant to be read at home, I will make it short, though
it will not be sweet, for I have not a sweet subject.[2]

The brevity of this present volume is, I pray, excused
on the same grounds in the hope that others will then
build on this foundation.

Deo soli gloria. Jesu Juva.

PART ONE

THE PRESENT AND HISTORY

Allah has bought from the Umma—the true believers of Islam—their selves and their substance in return for Paradise; they fight in the way of Allah, killing and being killed. Their promise is written in the blood of the moon. Rejoice in the bargain. That is surely the supreme triumph.

Koran 9:112

There was a great earthquake; and the sun became black as sackcloth made of hair, and the whole moon became like blood. The stars of the sky fell to the earth, as a fig tree casts its unripe fruit when shaken by a great wind. And the sky was split apart like a scroll when it is rolled up; and every mountain and island were moved out of their places. And the kings of the earth and the great men and the commanders and the rich and the strong and every slave and free man, hid themselves in the graves and among the rocks of the mountains; and they said to the mountains and to the rocks, "Fall on us and hide us from the presence of Him who sits on the throne, and from the wrath of the Lamb"; for the great day of their wrath has come; and who is able to stand?

Revelation 6:12–17

CHAPTER ONE

AS THE MOON RISES AND SETS: PRELUDE TO WAR

The greatest advances in human civilization have come when we recovered what we had lost: when we learned the lessons of history.

Winston Churchill

Great and marvelous are Your deeds, Lord God Almighty. Just and true are your ways, King of the Ages. Who will not fear you, O Lord, and give glory to Your Name?

Revelation 15:3–4

Within a matter of weeks three different countries in the Middle East were invaded by neighboring nations. Their governments were displaced, their people were dispossessed, and their resources were dissipated. When Syria overran Lebanon, the world barely noticed. When Libya led a coup in Chad, the incident was almost entirely overlooked. But when Iraq swept into Kuwait, an international crisis—and ultimately war—was provoked. Why? What made the difference?

Iraq's antics in the region are not exactly unprecedented. The conflict between Kuwait and Iraq has flared up again and again over the past thirty years, resulting in armed confrontation on at least five occasions. In 1961 and again in 1973, Iraq actually annexed portions of its tiny gulf

7

neighbor. Why, then, was the intelligence community in the United States so surprised when the old rivalry resurfaced in 1990? And why the dramatic reaction?

World attention has been focused for months on the Palestinian resistance movement, or *Intifada,* in Israel's occupied West Bank and Gaza territories. Images of armed Israeli military forces engaging rock-throwing children in combat have been etched in the minds of television viewers around the globe. But even as the tide of world opinion turns against Israel, the many other *Intifadas* throughout the region are virtually ignored—the *Intifada* of the Kurds in Iraq, the *Intifada* of the Shiites in Tajukskaya, the *Intifada* of the Albanian Moslems in Kossovo, the *Intifada* of the Druze in Lebanon, the *Intifada* of the Azaria in Azarbidjan, the *Intifada* of the Sunni in Kashmir, the *Intifada* of the Armenians in Turkey, the *Intifada* of the Dinka in Sudan, and the *Intifada* of the Copts in Egypt. Why is one uprising front page news when all the others constitute no news at all?

In Iran, the home of Islamic fundamentalism, the excavation and restoration of the ancient ruins of pagan Persia have become a national priority. Likewise, in Syria, Iraq, Saudi Arabia, Algeria, Libya, Jordan, and Egypt—each a very strict Moslem state—the artifacts and achievements of their pre-Moslem forbears have become rallying points for both national patriotism and pan-Arab pride. Why this odd lapse of piety and consistency?

The international enthusiasts of *Détente, Glastnost,* and *Perestroika* have happily abandoned their earlier predictions of an era of peace and cooperation. They now mobilize huge multinational forces to decisively crush any possible threat to their freshly refurbished New World Order. Why the sudden turnaround?

The answer to each of these important questions will not be found in State Department dossiers. They will not be disclosed in classified Pentagon reports. They will not be revealed in White House press briefings. And they certainly will not be related in the dispatches of the popular media. Instead, the answers to these questions, surely the most plaguing dilemmas of the present and perhaps of the future, may only be found in the past. The answers to these questions are only divulged in the seldom-consulted annals of history.

      ੴ   ੴ   ੴ

"History is bunk."[1] When Henry Ford said that, he was not only stating an opinion about his least favorite subject in school; he was expressing an American state of mind. We are not particularly fond of the musty dusty past. And whatever fascinations we may continue to harbor, we relegate to the realms of sentiment or nostalgia.

As the renowned historian, Daniel Boorstin, has pointed out:

> In our schools today, the story of our nation has been replaced by *social studies*—which is the study of what ails us *now*. In our churches, the effort to see the essential nature of man has been displaced by the *social gospel*— which is the polemic against the pet vices of *today*. Our book publishers no longer seek the timeless and the durable, but spend most of their efforts in a fruitless search for—*la mode social commentary*—which they pray will not be out of date when the item goes to press. Our merchandisers frantically devise their new year models, which will cease to be voguish when their sequels appear three months hence. Neither our classroom lessons nor our sermons nor our books nor the things we live with nor the houses we live in are any longer strong ties to our past.[2]

The result, according to Boorstin, is that

> We have become a nation of short-term doomsayers. In a word, we have lost our sense of history. Without the materials of historical comparison, we are left with nothing but abstractions.[3]

It seems that in our mad rush toward a New World Order we have become afflicted with a malignant contemporaneity. Our morbid preoccupation with ourselves, and thus our ambivalence and ignorance of the past, has trapped us in a recalcitrant present.

The fact is, history is not just the concern of historians and social scientists. It is not the lonely domain of political prognosticators and ivory tower academics. It is the very stuff of life.

In the volatile, headline-grabbing Middle East, for instance, the importance of history is obvious to even the most casual observer. Not only is the region steeped in glorious traditions that reach back to the very dawning of civilization; but more often than not, it is still governed by those ancient ambitions and rivalries. Israelis tenaciously hold on to the occupied territories of the West Bank because of promises made millenniums ago to the patriarch Abraham; Iraqis invade the lands of fellow Moslems in order to settle grudges that date back to the time of Nebuchadnezzar; Iranians stir up revolutionary passions that have lain dormant since the demise of Ali and Hussein late in the seventh century; and Egyptians, recalling the former glory of pharaohs and pyramids, issue calls for a revitalized military and a pan-Arab revival of their former empire.

The crisis in the Middle East is, of course, terribly complex. It involves questions of geo-political security, national sovereignty, racial rancor, religious contention, and military prowess. But central to each of these questions is the primordial importance of history. Even the question of prophetic fulfillment revolves around various historical concerns. After all, the prophetic passages of the Bible are inextricably linked to the peoples, issues, and events of those ancient times when they were first recorded under the superintendence of our sovereign God. Prophecy is, in fact, simply *history foretold*—utilizing the same structure, language, and facility of *history retold*.

In addition, Biblical prophecy is fulfilled in at least three ways in history. There is an initial fulfillment. There is a continual fulfillment. And there is an ultimate fulfillment. Therefore, understanding how prophecy *has been* fulfilled is the most important key to understanding how prophecy *will be* fulfilled.

There can be little doubt, then, that understanding the past is the key to understanding the future. Especially when it comes to the Middle East, to ignore history is to invite disaster.

If we are to negotiate the dangerous shoals of Middle Eastern diplomacy with any degree of success, we cannot simply match our adversaries army for army and missile for missile. We cannot responsibly hope to bring resolve to eons-old conflicts if we do not comprehend their roots. As David R. Carlin has said:

> The best way to develop an attitude of responsibility toward the future is to cultivate a sense of responsibility toward the past. We are born into a world that we didn't make, and it is only fair that we should be grateful to those who did make it. Such gratitude carries with it the imperative that we preserve and at least slightly improve the world that has been given us before passing it on to subsequent generations. We stand in the midst of many generations. If we are indifferent to those who went before us and actually existed, how can we expect to be concerned for the well-being of those who come after us and only potentially exist.[4]

The aim of this book is thus quite simple: to shed a little light on the perilous present and the frightening future by shedding a little light on the ponderous past. I have not tried to plot either a diplomatic or a military solution. I have not tried to decode the prophetic destiny of the region. I have only attempted to remind us all of some long forgotten facts of history—to expose the roots of the crisis. I can only hope that, in the process, I will be able to help provoke a new attitude of responsibility—and to help us avoid the disaster that always awaits the oblivious. After all, the Bible clearly states that:

> Wonders cannot be known in the midst of darkness.
> Righteousness cannot be done in a land of forgetfulness.
> (Psalm 88:12)

CHAPTER TWO

THE ELEVENTH PLAGUE: THIS PRESENT CRISIS

We believe that because we are on the side of truth, then we are on the side of God. And because God is with us, then everything shall be in our favor.

Saddam Hussein

Know this, that in the last days perilous times will come: For men will be lovers of themselves, lovers of money, boasters, proud, blasphemers, disobedient to parents, unthankful, unholy, unloving, unforgiving, slanderers, without self-control, brutal, despisers of good, traitors, headstrong, haughty, lovers of pleasure rather than lovers of God, having a form of godliness but denying its power. . . . As Jannes and Jambres resisted Moses, so do these also resist the truth: men of corrupt minds, disapproved concerning the faith; but they will progress no further.

2 Timothy 3:1–5, 8–9, NKJV

Like man himself, this land is an enigma.
The cradle of civilization, the wellspring of faith, the powder keg of ardor, and the terminus of time—there is no other place on earth where so much has occurred for so long and affected so many. The Middle East is the ominous, swarthy, and mysterious hinge upon which, it seems, all of history turns. Alternately rocked by unending wars

and soothed by undying devotion, tortured by unflinching fanaticism and calmed by unyielding patience, this small crescent of sand and stone is once again the stage upon which the passion play of mankind's trauma is set—where war is waged for the sake of peace, where hatred is stoked for the sake of righteousness, and where tyranny is invoked for the sake of freedom.

The swirling dust clouds just above the surface of the desert give the amber lamps of military caravans the gauzy glow of distant planets. The long lines of men and armaments are hardly an uncommon sight here. Before the American troops had ever established their bivouacs, the British, the French, the Turks, the Saracens, the Crusaders, the Mongols, the Greeks, the Romans, the Byzantines, the Persians, the Egyptians, the Sumerians, the Babylonians, and the Assyrians had also passed this way. Even so, the landscape has never lost its etherial and unearthly look. This ancient bridge between the two worlds of East and West—common to every resurgent ambition—is yet alien to man. And so it shall ever be.

"You really feel your mortality here," Mark Edwards told me. Stationed in the Saudi desert near Riyadh, Mark was a part of the first wave of troops sent in to face down the aggression of Saddam Hussein. "Just north of here, Alexander the Great confronted Darius in 331 B.C. Over to the west, Saladin met Richard the Lionhearted in A.D. 1191. Just over the horizon there, Napoleon was turned back by Laraturk in 1798. They've all come and gone. And the desert wind and the passing time have covered their tracks without a trace. It's almost as if they had never been here at all. Now here we are, in the same place, fighting the same battles for the same reasons."

He looked across the vast expanse of sandy crags and then shrugged in resignation. "But then, what's a guy gonna do? I'm in the Reserves because I want to serve my country. So, I don't take my duty lightly. But I'll tell you, it was hard saying good-bye to my wife and children. Really hard. This was our daughter's first Christmas. We'd moved into a new neighborhood. I'd just gotten promoted to supervisor at the plant. Things really seemed to be going well for us. And then this."

He told me about several of the men he had met in the camp—men who, like Mark, had left homes and families, jobs, hopes, and dreams to come to this faraway alien land. "Each of us is ready to fight," he said. "And we're quite confident we can win. Hands down. But we can't help but wonder why—and if it'll make any difference. But then I guess those are the questions that come up in any war. And there is nothing we can do—win, lose, or draw—about the desert wind or the passing of time. Nothing except pray."

Then, with wry irony in his voice, he added, "The problem is, we can't even pray all that often for fear of offending the Saudis."

ॐ   ॐ   ॐ

It was William Blake who first gave the name *Jerusalem* to all that was tender and lovely in the human soul. He wrote of her as a beautiful woman who maintains her virtue despite the indignities imposed by the ages. He described her as a pristine kingdom whose true spirit has fallen asleep but will not die, despite the decline of man and his ignominious fall. Blake's poetic instinct grasped the truth that this city, more than any other, has always paradigmically nourished sincere holiness—and sincere betrayal.

Here, where the present is but a gossamer above ages past, history is inescapable. It hangs in the air like the wail of the faithful before the Western Wall. It intrudes on every conversation like the wheedling cries of Arab merchants at the Jaffa gate. It pierces every waking moment like the glinting gold of the *Haram es Sherif* against the Judean sky.

And yet, the gossamer is thick and dull.

"The past is the air that we breathe and the hope that we cling to," Uldi Salreageini told me. "But the present is the awful necessity that we must live with—holy places guarded with automatic weapons, ancient relics marred by political posturing, centuries-old streets with security police careening along in armored vehicles, and the quietude of prayer disturbed by the wail of sirens and the angry cries of the *Intifada*. Such things ought not to be. But alas, so it has been throughout time. Someone has said that the constant presence of strife is not an interruption of Jerusalem's historical charm—it *is* Jerusalem's historical charm. Still, it is more than a little disturbing."

To emerge from the architectural and acoustical marvels within the Church of Saint Anne, built by the Crusaders just adjacent to the five porticoes of the Pool of Bethesda, only to be confronted with *uzi*-bearing soldiers is indeed discomfiting and disorienting. To pray in the Church of the Holy Sepulcher before Golgotha under the watchful eyes of security police with walkie-talkies is likewise a strange anomaly. To wander down the *Via Dolorosa* recalling the chronology of the Gospel accounts of the passion of Christ Jesus, with the angry anarchy of the Saracen Quarter as a backdrop, is surely somehow misplaced and misbegotten.

But then, that is Jerusalem as much as the glorious view from the Mount of Olives or the dust swirling through the crowded streets along the Kidron Valley, as much as the quietude of Gordon's Garden Tomb or the frenzied bustle around the Damascus Gate, as much as the intensity of *Shabat* or the solemnity of *Ramadan*.

"We came here for a taste of peace," Uldi told me. "But we have supped only on war. I myself have fought in every war since 1948. My sons fought in 1973. Now my grandchildren are in the military. Last month, all three generations served together in exercises in the Golan Heights. Can you believe it? An old man and his grandchildren serving together in war?"

Flipping open his small, worn copy of the Torah, he showed me the place where Moses promised the people of the covenant that they would never again be afflicted by the diseases and plagues of Egypt if only they would obey the Lord in every detail of their lives. "Some say that this plague of continual violence and upheaval, worse than all of the ten that afflicted Egypt, is our recompense for un-righteousness."

He turned to me with tears streaking his leathery brown cheeks. "I just wish the madness could end. I just wish that this eleventh plague would pass. Somehow. Some-way. Sometime. I am tired. We all are. Pray for the peace of Jerusalem. Won't you?"

             🍂   🍂   🍂

"We are in a no-win situation," Michael al Jerash told me. "Truly, we are between a rock and a hard place. The rock is pan-Arab Islam. The hard place is the West. If we please one, we alienate the other. If we straddle the line between the two, we will be crushed by both. No matter where the battle lines are drawn, we will be caught in the middle. We will lose. That is the dilemma of Jordan in general—and of Arab Christians here in particular."

His piercing Bedouin eyes scanned the scene in front of him—one of the many lively *Souqs* not far from the fa-bled Qasr Khareneh Citadel. The marketplace was a warren of alleyways filled with the frantic clutter of merchants hawking their wares—intricate *narguilah* pipes; copper-stud-ded *zanzibar* chests; tall, exotic *hookahs;* richly embroidered *khaimah* textiles; ornate *hufuf* pottery; jewel-encrusted *khanjar* knives; antique *dillah* coffee pots; and deep iron *mihmahs* skillets.

"My family first came here from Cilicia at the beginning of the second century," he said. "The Roman settlement—which was at that time called Philadelphia—had a dynamic Christian community that, according to our tradition, was the recipient of Saint John's sole gracious pastoral letter in all of the *Apocalypsion*. My forefathers lived as a persecuted minority under the successive rules of the Byzantines, the Sassanids, the Umayyads, the Saljuks, the Ottomans, the British, and now the Hashemites. But this most recent threat is the gravest of all."

As we walked toward *Jebel al Qalat,* the harsh noon sun, like muted moonlight, put to sleep the colors. There were only bright splashes of light and deep, foreboding shadows. The streets became a monochromatic maze. "Our region has been anything but stable in recent years," he said. "King Abdullah was assassinated in 1951. King Talal was forced to abdicate a little more than a year later. And King Hussein has suffered at least five attempts on his life and three concerted coups. But with the constriction we face today, there is really no telling how, or if, we will be able to survive. And we Christians are likely to suffer the brunt of whatever scenario plays its course here. We are the forgotten element of this whole dilemma."

He stopped and asked, as much to himself as to me, "Do you think the church in the West will remember us? Is there any ground for hope? Or will war swallow us up once again?"

ꙮ   ꙮ   ꙮ

The woman on the other end of the phone line was agitated. She told me that the trouble had begun in church—which is, of course, a profound assessment of both historical and Biblical theology. After some time, the whole story came out.

"Clearly, we are in the Last Days," the guest speaker at her church had said. "The signs of the times are indisputable. Jesus is coming soon. We can expect to see the Rapture of the church, the Great Tribulation, the mark of the Beast, the reign of the Antichrist, the revival of the Roman Empire, the Battle of Armageddon, and the initiation of the Millennium—all within this very generation."

His eloquence held the congregation in rapt attention. With authority he quoted supporting verses, spouted vital statistics, and reiterated significant dates. He referred to maps, charts, slides, and timelines all luminously projected on the screen behind the pulpit. For more than an hour he explained how the events currently splashed across the world's headlines were specifically predicted in the Bible thousands of years before.

And he was a man to be believed. He was an expert on the subject of prophecy, after all—a tenured professor at one of the most respected evangelical seminaries in America.

Even so, after the service the congregation was abuzz. In this town, where more than twenty thousand troops had been stationed until the military buildup in the Saudi desert, any discussion of the Middle East was certain to stoke the fires of interest and concern. Out in the parking lot, the wives and children, the parents and loved ones, and the friends and neighbors of the participants in Operation Desert Storm mulled over the implications of the sermon in tense knots of conversation.

"I have to tell you, I'm more confused than ever," one man volunteered in frustration. "All this business about killer bees and cobra helicopters is a bit much for me."

"Well, it's a matter of interpretation, really," answered another. "You have to know what to look for—how to decipher Scripture's ancient imagery."

"I know. But I've been hearing this stuff all my life. The same charts. The same maps. The same scenarios. Only the dates change—they keep having to push them back. It just gets more and more inconclusive as the years roll on and the system gets more and more convoluted. Always doomsaying."

"But, the Bible says . . . "

"No now, don't get me wrong. I'm not questioning the Bible. Not at all. But you said yourself that it's all a matter of interpretation. I just have to wonder if we're not kind of baptizing the headlines onto the Bible instead of the other way around."

"All I know or care about is that my husband is right in the middle of what may or may not be an awful conflagration," a young mother interjected. "I'm not sure how relevant prophecy is to me and my children right now. I'm just trying to walk with Christ moment by moment—to keep our heads above water and our family functioning. I'm looking to the Scriptures for wisdom and direction as well as for comfort."

"I don't know if these are the end times," responded another. "But I'm not so sure it really matters. I do know that God is sovereign and that He's given us a job to do. Whether there are hitchhiking angels in Southern California or Beast-coded Social Security checks in New Hampshire or demon-controlled master computers in Belgium is another matter altogether. The Bible informs us so that we can do what God wants us to do and so that we can be what God wants us to be."

"Well, I'm not sure what to believe either," said still another. "I can't decide whether I should be terrified or excited. I think I'm just confused."

"I just wish I understood better why all this is happening in the Middle East and how the Bible applies—without the spectacularization," the first man said. "I'd like to know why my son's life is on the line right now."

"Amen to that," the others concurred.

❧   ❧   ❧

Once upon a time, all of the citizens of Kuwait were as rich as kings. They reveled in opulence. They built themselves villas overlooking the coast out of frosty Italian marble. They bought automobiles and airplanes and sophisticated electronics like they were toys. They had no taxes to worry them. Education was free. So was medical care. Their capitol rose up out of a sandy wasteland gleaming like Epcott and resplendent like Versailles. Their vast shopping mall, the Sultan Center, was open twenty-four hours a day, seven days a week, all year round, except during Ramadan. There they could sample the finest French cuisine, the latest Italian designs, the cleverest Japanese consumer goods, and the latest American pop phenomena. There was even an ice skating rink—an unheard of luxury in the parched environs of the Persian Gulf.

"Looking back now, it seems like utopia," Hikmat al Khalil told me.

Before the invasion of this never-never land by Iraqi forces in the summer of 1990, Hikmat was a prosperous importer of Norwegian salmon and Russian caviar. His harrowing escape through the desert is the stuff of legend.

"Fortunately, when the tanks rolled in, our whole family was together, " he explained. "When it became apparent that our defensive forces were hopelessly overpowered, we began making plans for our escape. We loaded our small family car with as many of our personal things as we could carry and struck out toward Saudi—or Abu Dhabi or Bahrain or the Emirates or wherever. We just wanted to get out."

The all-night drive across arid dunes and basalt hills was fraught with danger. Three times Hikmat was turned back by Iraqi patrols. Once he was held up for three hours at a hastily constructed check-station near the border while his wife and children were interrogated at gunpoint. Explosive blasts ripped the desolate desert silence and lit the night sky.

"I have never before been as frightened as I was that night," he said. "Somehow, we finally got through. Our car was nearly out of gas. Everything I had worked for was gone. But we were alive. And free."

After a long pause he continued, "I was so relieved then. But now all I can think about is getting back in, reclaiming what is rightfully ours, going home."

He looked down at his watch and suddenly realized it was time for his evening prayers. He bid me farewell and then turned his face to the East, where his haunting incantation wafted upward toward the blood of the moon.

PART TWO

THE PAST
AND PROPHECY

I am the wound and the knife. I am the blow and the cheek. I am the limbs and the wheel. I am the victim and the executioner.

Les Fleurs du Mal

I will show wonders in the heavens and in the earth; blood and fire and pillars of smoke. The sun shall be turned into darkness, and the moon into blood, before the coming of the great and terrible day of the Lord. And it shall come to pass that whoever calls on the name of the Lord shall be saved.

Joel 2:30–31, NKJV

CHAPTER THREE

THE SONS OF HAM: ANCIENT EMPIRES AND RECURRING DREAMS

Love, friendship, and respect do not unite people as much as a common hatred for something.

Anton Chekhov

This is the interpretation of the prophecy. Mene: *God has numbered your kingdom and finished it;* Tekel: *You have been weighed in the balances and been found wanting;* Peres: *Your kingdom has been divided and given over.*

Daniel 5:26–28

All of Iraq's most prominent Islamic leaders representing virtually every variant branch of that stern eclectic faith—from the Sunnis to the Shiites, from the Zaydis to the Ismailis, from the Sufis to Wahhabis, from the Marabouts to the Senussi, and from the Druze to the Alawites—were present at the lavish pagan festival. But there were no cries of outrage, no sworn condemnations, no blasphemies. The entire event was taken very much in stride. It was, after all, a day of national pride—a rare opportunity for them to come together acknowledging their common roots. They conferred on it their wholehearted *Ijma*—their unanimous approval.

It was the festival of the ancient Mesopotamian goddess of fertility, Ishtar. Celebrated in a newly consecrated temple district, it was to be the centerpiece of Saddam Hussein's week-long revelry. It commemorated the end of his bloody, costly conflict with Iran in 1989.

The bronze talisman of Ishtar, a faithful reproduction of an ancient idol from the time of Nebuchadnezzar, was unveiled. Incense bathed the entire vicinity with an air of sanctity. Ethereal music lilted in the breeze. Costumed attendants bearing torches led a long processional in a triumphant march. Then, as if this were the moment they had all been waiting for, Saddam Hussein stepped onto a strobe-lit platform and announced the commencement of a New World Order, taking the ancient pledge of kings:

> I will wash my hands and my feet in the blood of the infidels for the glory of Mesopotamia forever.

The solemn clerics were pleased. The *Ji'had* had begun. The world would once again feel *Dar al Harb*—the scourge of war. Babylon was reborn.

Babylon

Sometime shortly after his debacle at Babel around 2250 B.C., Nimrod established several villages and trading centers all along the Euphrates River, including the city of Babylon. According to the Bible, Nimrod was a mighty and fearsome man who made those cultures in his own image (see Genesis 10:8–12). Thus, from its earliest days Babylon and its neighbors were known for their fierceness and aggression.

A long line of strong leaders enabled Babylon to gain preeminence over all the other settlements, building the city into an imperial power with dominions ultimately stretching from the Caspian to the Nile. Though the land surrounding it was always parched and poor, Babylon used

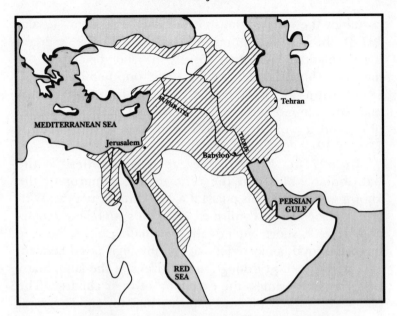

BABYLONIAN EMPIRE 550 B.C.

its military might to accumulate unfathomable riches. Its markets overflowed with the wealth and splendor of a thousand realms. Its profusion of magnificent architectural marvels—from the beautiful double-wide walls and crenelated towers to the broad processional avenues and multi-tiered temples—made it the envy of the world. Its fabled gates both awed and terrified adversaries. Its gardens, canals, and palaces dazzled visitors. Its art, literature, music, and religion set the standard for every other civilization in the ancient world. Though it suffered an occasional military humiliation or political setback at the hands of the Hittites, the Medes, the Persians, the Greeks, or even rival Mesopotamian settlements, Babylon remained the cultural and economic center of gravity in the region for nearly two millennia.

Both at home and abroad, the cruelly imposed Babylonian culture was perverse and depraved. In fact, throughout the Bible it epitomizes the essence of evil. Accordingly the city is variously called the "devastator" (Psalm 137:8), the "furious oppressor" (Isaiah 14:4), the "everlasting desolation" (Jeremiah 25:12), the "horror among the nations" (Jeremiah 50:23), and the "mother of harlots" (Revelation 17:5). It symbolizes the fountainhead of mankind's immorality, the wellspring of earth's abominations, and the object of God's wrath (see Revelation 14:8; 17:5; 16:19).

In 597 B.C. Nebuchadnezzar, the mightiest of the Babylonian kings and the renowned conqueror of the known world, swept his puissant armies into Jerusalem. With cruel efficiency he confirmed Babylon's merciless reputation. After a short but brutally debilitating siege, he captured the royal family of Jehoiachin, the high priest Seraiah, and all of the most distinguished citizens of the land. Many were forced to witness the execution of their children. The rest were dragged off into captivity in Babylon. The royal treasury was looted. The temple was ransacked and its treasures added to Nebuchadnezzar's booty. And as a final indignity, many of the survivors were driven penniless from their homes into foreign exile.

Eleven years later, in 586 B.C., Nebuchadnezzar again scourged Jerusalem. The puppet provincial government he had installed under Zedekiah had shown signs of unrest, so the Babylonian monarch determined to put an end to the Jews once and for all. A massacre followed. Rapine and destruction were unrestrained. The temple was destroyed. The royal palace and the city were set ablaze and the last of the bedraggled inhabitants deported. The prophets Ezekiel and Jeremiah recorded the awful event with grievous clarity. Clearly, the spirit and character of imperial Babylon had been disclosed.

After Nebuchadnezzar, the city began a precipitous decline and was finally destroyed and depopulated, in fulfillment of innumerable prophecies in Scripture. But the spirit of Babylon was not forgotten. In fact, the dream of reviving Babylonian glory has haunted Mesopotamia, the region we now call Iraq, ever since. In modern times, that yearning has propelled Nebuchadnezzar's progeny into one insane war after another. After the moderate young Hashemite king Feisal was assassinated in 1958, Iraqi leaders carefully followed the old empire's primeval prescription for conquest: attacking their ancient foe Israel in 1967 and 1973, invading the Kuwaiti heirs of their Mesopotamian rivals Sumer and Akkad in 1961, 1973, and 1990, and engaging their primordial Persian enemies in Iran in a devastating, protracted war from 1980 to 1988.

Early in his tenure, Saddam Hussein announced his intentions to restore Iraq's Babylonian heritage. He launched a meticulous, multi-billion-dollar excavation and reconstruction of the ancient city located sixty miles south of Baghdad, rebuilding a number of its most significant sites. They included Nebuchadnezzar's opulent grand palace, the vast Esagila temple precinct, the beautiful Via Sacra processional boulevard, and the resplendent hanging gardens of the Lugalgirra District. In addition, he rewrote the Iraqi constitution to mirror that of Hammurabi. He reformed the bureaucracy to emulate that of Merodachbaladan. He restructured the military to mimic that of Nabopolassar. He even revived academic and experimental interests in the cult of Ishtar, Babylon's ancient fertility religion that combined many of the elements of what we today call the New Age Movement with various ancient pagan rituals.

Hussein fully embraced the spirit of Babylon with an unapologetic, messianic fervor. At the dedication of the newly reconstructed Ishtar Gate he said:

> Glorious in a glorious time, Babylon is the lady of reviving centuries, rising dignified and holy, showing the great history of Iraq. Added to its magnificence and emphasizing its originality, the phoenix of the new time rises alive from the ashes of the past to face the bright present—thus placing it on a golden throne, bringing back its charm, its charming youth, and unique glory.

Babylon is not a city made of rocks and bricks—full of
mere human events. It is not a forgotten place of the
ancient past. Babylon is something else altogether. Since
its birth, Babylon has stretched out its arms to the future—to be the seat of eternal wisdom, to represent the
first civilization, and to remain as the glittering light-
house in the dark night of history. Here is Babylon.[1]

The implications of these Babylonian ambitions were
made plain in an official Iraqi publication which asserted
that:

Saddam Hussein has emerged from Mesopotamia as did
Hammurabi, as did Merodachbaladan, and as did
Nebuchadnezzar. He has emerged at a time to shake the
centuries-old dust off Babylon's face. History must start
with us so that Babylon can remain mankind's compass
throughout the ages. Spirit arise.[2]

The spirit of Babylon is not the only shade being con-
jured from the distant past in the Middle East. Throughout
the region, the legacy of ancient glory is proving to be an
irresistible catalyst for nationalistic fervor.

Assyria

At the northern end of the valley between the Tigris and
Euphrates rivers, the city of Nineveh, like Babylon, was established by Nimrod sometime after the dispersion at
Babel. Although it quickly became an important commercial center, it failed to build a lasting empire of any sort for
more than fifteen hundred years.

Throughout those years, the city-state was generally
dominated politically and militarily by Babylon; but somehow it still maintained its own cultural identity. And because it lay along the primary trade routes, north to the
Caspian and west to the Mediterranean, it developed an
independent source of income. Over time, Nineveh became a huge metropolis with more than 120,000 residents.

Though its architecture tended to be drab and utilitarian, it was impressive by its sheer bulk. Its gargantuan walls, for instance, were wide enough for chariots to race twelve abreast along the top. Its homes were fairly nondescript but commodious and well designed for extended family life. It did produce a large body of literature and an array of creative arts, but most of the efforts seemed to be devoted to commercial or bureaucratic themes. Even its paganism was rather sedate compared to its raucous neighbors. Ninevah was, in short, a quiet and stable community.

By 800 B.C. it seemed poised to finally emerge from the shadow of its more flamboyant southern neighbor, Babylon. That was about the time, the Bible records, that the prophet Jonah made his reluctant visit to Nineveh. After traversing the length of the city for three days fiercely preaching the judgment of God and repentance from wickedness, he met with unprecedented success:

> The people of Nineveh believed God, proclaimed a fast, and put on sackcloth, from the greatest to the least of them. Then the Word came to the king of Nineveh; and he arose from his throne and laid aside his robe, covered himself with sackcloth and sat in ashes. And he caused it to be proclaimed and published throughout Nineveh by the decree of the king and his nobles, saying: "Let neither man nor beast, herd nor flock, taste anything; do not let them eat or drink water. But let man and beast be covered with sackcloth, and cry mightily to God; yes, let every one turn from his evil way and from the violence that is in his hands. Who can tell if God will turn and relent, and turn away from His fierce anger, so that we may not perish?" (Jonah 3:5–9, NKJV)

Following this dramatic conversion of all the Assyrian people—from the highest to the lowest, including their young king, Adadnirari—God indeed relented and spared the city. And it would never be the same again.

According to the Bible, conversion is not simply an ethical or philosophical revision. It is a transformation of the very soul. It affects every detail of life. A converted individual is altogether different than he was before. He has new motivations, new standards, and new objectives. He has a new outlook, a new way of thinking, and a new way of living. He is born anew (see 2 Corinthians 5:17).

In the same way, when a culture is converted, it too is transformed. The old disappears. The new is ushered in. Covenantal faithfulness and obedience replace covenantal rebellion and insubordination. Integrity, diligence, and productivity supplant corruption, deceit, and sloth. God's blessing covers the curse of sin (see Deuteronomy 28:1–14).

This being the case, it is not surprising to see dramatic changes in the nature of Assyrian society. Apparently, the three kings that immediately followed Adadnirari—Shalmanesar, Asshurdan, and Asshurnirari—followed his example and walked in obedience to the Lord. They entered into a warm relationship with the kingdoms of Israel and Judah (see 2 Kings 12–15; 2 Chronicles 24–28), and tremendous wealth and power began to flow into the city. In a very short period of time Assyria began to dominate the entire region.

Suddenly, like a bolt out of the blue, Assyrian civilization began to flower. Economic, political, and military prowess was matched with artistic, literary, and architectural splendor. The desert bloomed as better agricultural methods were applied. Breakthrough innovations spawned new marvels of engineering. Peace and prosperity prevailed.

Sadly, this blessed state was short-lived. Pride gave way to apostasy. Tiglathpilezor attempted to synthesize the old paganism with faith in Jehovah. Driven more by political ambition than by theological heterodoxy, he wanted to consolidate his control on his growing empire. So long as the temple in Jerusalem remained a rival focus of affection and loyalty in the hearts and minds of his people, his security was undermined. So he diverted the locus of worship to Nineveh and the old cultus.

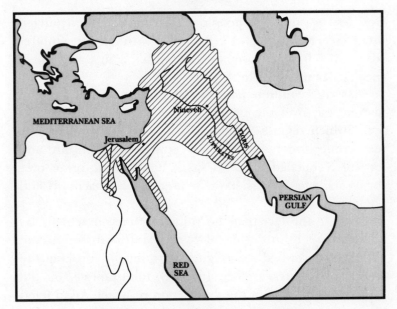

ASSYRIAN EMPIRE 700 B.C.

By the time of Shalmaneser's dynasty, the wealth and power that God had graciously bestowed on Assyria had been harnessed for wickedness. Tilgathpilezor's polyglot theology had wrought a bitter harvest. Tyranny, brutality, and aggression were unleashed on the subjected lands of the empire. In 722, the kingdom of Israel was overrun and its people dispossessed. Later, under Sennacherib, even Jerusalem was sieged. Throughout this time, the Assyrians demonstrated their familiarity with the Biblical covenant but continued their refusal to submit to it (see Isaiah 36:10–20).

What Tiglathpilezar, Shalmaneser, and Sennacherib failed to recognize is that with covenantal blessing comes covenantal responsibility (see Deuteronomy 28:15–68). To whom much is given, much is required (see Luke 12:48). God disciplines His prodigals, even to the point of destruction (see Hebrews 12:5–6; Ezekiel 31:3–16). As a result,

God first warned the people of Assyria and then judged them (see Nahum 1:1-15; 3:12-19). While other empires rose and fell slowly over time, Assyria's course was like a spectacular spent rocket.

Assyria's sudden power and influence still holds a mythic sway over the people of the region, particularly in Syria, which regards itself as the heir to Nineveh's legacy. Just as the leaders of Iraq have appealed to the lure and lore of Nebuchadnezzar to spark nationalistic pride over the years, the Syrians have focused on Sennacherib and Shalmaneser.

Despite the fact that the ruins of Nineveh actually lay outside the boundaries of Syria, Hafez al Assad, the nation's uncrowned sovereign, is continually invoking the memory of Assyria's glory. In 1978, for example, on the 2,750th anniversary of the destruction of Israel, Assad feted his close-knit Alawite community with a lavish celebration that lasted a full week. No expense was spared. The richest foods, the most exotic entertainments, and the most earthly pleasures were provided without end. The days were spent in revelry, the nights in debauchery. Speech making and ribald *Braggadocio* punctuated the hours. Finally, a solid gold statue of the ancient Assyrian deity, Ashur, was ritually dedicated with Islamic *Shahadas* and *Rakatins*.

At the height of the celebration, Assad summarized his Assyrian ambitions for the future:

> We are the heirs of Sennacherib and Shalmaneser—the greatest heroes of our nation. We have inherited their glory. We have inherited their wisdom. We have inherited their valor. But most of all, we have inherited their cause. Assyria must once again unite the Arab world against the imperialism of the Infidel, the interloping of the West, and the encroachment of the Jew.[3]

He concluded the grand event by saying:

Assyria must arise and conquer. Nothing must be able to stand in our path. Indeed nothing can stand in our path. The world is once again divided between *Dar al Islam*—the abode of faith—and *Dar al Harb*—the abode of war. Like Sennacherib, we shall sweep aside every obstacle. Like him, we shall prevail. *Ji'had. Insh'allah.*[4]

Persia

In 539 B.C. an alliance of Medes and Persians—the Mongol and Parthavian peoples of Kurdistan and the Farsi and Elamite peoples of Iran—swept across the Middle East, conquering both Babylonia and Assyria. After two thousand years of uninterrupted Arab rule, the Middle East had fallen into the hands of alien conquerors, thus perfectly fulfilling the prophecies of Isaiah, Jeremiah, Ezekiel, Daniel, Habakkuk, and Nahum.

The Persian rulers, from Cyrus to Xerxes and Darius to Artaxerxes, were refined and benevolent. Their culture was extravagant and cosmopolitan, and they reveled in sleek modernity. They exercised compassion on their captive peoples, allowing the Jews to return to Jerusalem under Ezra and Nehemiah, for instance. And they were ecumenical in their religious tolerance. Only in their hunger for military might and territorial conquest was their fierceness revealed.

At its zenith, their empire was the largest of the ancient world, covering almost double the territory of Babylonia and triple the territory of Assyria. Their wealth, too, outstripped anything else the world had ever seen. In addition, they were able to maintain control over their domain for nearly two millennia, save for the rude interruption of the Mongols during the thirteenth century.

Although technically part of the Middle East, the Persian kings distinguished themselves from their Arab brethren. They preserved their Farsi language rather than adopting the Arabic common to all of the other nations in the region. They emphasized their refined urban culture over and above the rough and tumble Bedouin mentality of their neighbors. And even after they were converted to Islam from Zoroastrianism during the seventh century, they maintained their dualistic mysticism and became the influential revolutionary center for both the Shiite and Wahhabi sects of fundamentalist Islam. As the ruling Pahlevi Shahs often asserted, the Persians were "a people apart."

Despite the constitutional establishment of modern Iran after World War I in place of the old Persia, the imperial ambitions of the people did not wane. They longed for the glory of the bygone era. They chafed against the yoke of Third World mediocrity. Then, providentially, the stream of wealth that came from Persian Gulf oil enabled them to stoke the fires of pride once again.

Thus, between 1967 and 1971, the Shah staged a series of Persian celebrations, including a lavish imperial coronation for himself, during a five-year-long observance of the twenty-five hundredth anniversary of the reign of Cyrus from Persepolis. These affairs turned out to be the most extravagant the modern world had ever witnessed—certainly worthy of the heir of Cyrus, Xerxes, Darius, and Artaxerxes!

The mantle that the Shah wore during the festivities was a gift from the people of Meshed and Khnassan. The long white cashmere garment was emblazoned with peacock feathers sewn with gold thread and pearls; and the edges, pockets, and sleeves were encrusted with gold and silver pailettes. The pearls alone weighed almost five pounds. The closing at the neck was an aigrette of diamonds set around one large emerald and five smaller, pear-shaped rubies—the gems arranged to resemble flags, banners, and ancient armaments. This extraordinary confection weighed nearly eight hundred carats. Around his waist the monarch wore a belt of gold mail with a buckle set with a huge two-hundred-carat emerald surrounded by sixty brilliants and nearly one hundred fifty diamonds. His

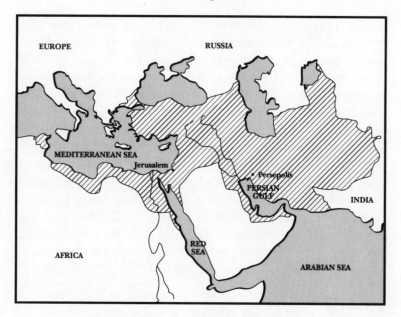

PERSIAN EMPIRE 400 B.C.

gold scepter, a gift from the people of Azerbaijan, was surmounted by a globe with three lions, three suns, and a crown of gold set with precious stones. His golden sword was slid into a sheath set with countless emeralds, rubies, sapphires, and more than twelve thousand diamonds. And his crown had more than three thousand diamonds, four hundred pearls, and a scattering of emeralds and sapphires.

Nearly two hundred acres of the ruins at Persepolis had been restored for the celebrations, great hangings of embossed purple velvet and gilt bronze friezes adorning every surface. The Shah was transported around the grounds in an ebony carriage encrusted with mother of pearl and stamped with the royal Persian crest. The dias that he sat upon was a replica of the famed peacock throne of Xerxes, made of gold-plated acacia wood set with nearly thirty thousand precious gemstones.

On one occasion nine kings, five queens, thirteen princes, eight princesses, sixteen presidents, three prime ministers, two governor generals, nine sheiks, and two sultans—more accumulated royalty than at any other time in history except at the funeral of Edward VII in 1910—gathered together for a grand banquet. The Shah served them a remarkable Persian feast of quail eggs stuffed with caviar, lobster mousse with *sause nantua,* flaming lambs with *arak,* roast peacock stuffed with *foie gras,* platters of cheese, a salad of figs and raspberries, champagne sherbet, twenty-five thousand bottles of wine, and a single seventy-pound cake.

Like the festival of Saddam Hussein in Babylon and the fete of Hafez al Assad in Deir ez Zur, the Shah's royal gala was designed to set the course for the future of the nation according to the compass of the past. According to the Shah:

> The glory of Persia is merely represented in the embellishments you see about you. In fact, the essence of that glory is yet to be fully realized as our nation only now begins to assume its proper place among the great nations of the earth. Persia shall arise.[5]

After the Shah was deposed by the stern and ascetic Ayatollah Ruhollah Khomeini in 1979, it would have seemed logical that such imperial ambitions—and certainly such imperial opulence—would have been altogether shunned. But while the Ayatollah's revolution renounced the corruption of the Shah, it actually embraced the ideal of Persian hegemony—or Islamic universalism. For instance, on his visit to the great reinforced vault in the basement of the Bank Melli, where the Shah had kept the royal Persian treasury along with his own imperial baubles, the Ayatollah asserted:

> Now in the hands of the *Mullahs* and *Talabehs,* these symbols of our great heritage shall give new impetus to the export of our revolution. Soon the spirit of Allah will sweep the faithful *Umma* of the Persian hoards across the earth: first, Jerusalem will be liberated for prayer; then,

the Great Satan will be humiliated and crushed; and finally, our *Ji'had* will free the oppressed masses on every
continent.[6]

On another occasion he said:

Our land has always been the seed-bed of true freedom—even before the Prophet came to correct the er-
rors of time. Once again Persia shall lead the world as
before. Conquest through *Ji'had* shall be our deliverance
and our glory.[7]

Thus, archeological exploration and restoration has
continued unabated since the Ayatollah's revolution. If anything, the activity at various Persian ruins has actually increased.

The *Imams* understand only too well that an understanding of the past is the key to an understanding of the
future.

Islamic Ambitions

In Islamic Iraq: a celebration of the spirit of pagan Babylon. In Islamic Syria: a celebration of the spirit of pagan
Assyria. In Islamic Iran: a celebration of the spirit of pagan
Persia. And the pattern is repeated in other orthodox Islamic communities: in Egypt, in Libya, in Sudan, in Algiers,
and in Saudi Arabia.

At first glance, it would seem that the spirit of ancient
paganism with its odd mixture of greed, tyranny, idolatry,
and occultism would be roundly condemned by the clerical
Imams, the *Talabehs,* the *Mullahs,* the *Mu'adhdhin,* or the
Ayatollahs. But, in fact, two of the most passionate and fundamental ambitions of Islam enabled and even compelled
them to embrace the primordial paganism of Babylon, Assyria, and Persia.

The first ambition is Arab hegemony. Islamic tradition
teaches that the faith revealed to Mohammed was not a
new religion but was the oldest of all religions—an aborigi-

nal and natural form of monotheism. According to the Koran, Islam is the original and unadulterated religion of the Middle East from which all other religions, including Judaism and Christianity, eventually developed. The ancient variants of this nascent Arabian mysticism in Babylon, Assyria, and Persia are thus popularly amalgamated into the universal heritage of Islam, despite distortions by virtue of their antiquity.

The symbiotic polytheism of the Meccan region Hejaz, with the god Allah at the head of the pantheon, was absorbed by Mohammed into his Saracen system. Similarly, the ancient and revered *Ka'ba,* the huge rectangular reliquary in the Meccan sanctuary, was transformed from a pagan temple into the focus of Moslem pilgrimage, the *Hadj.* The stories of Abraham, Moses, and Jesus were transferred from the Bible, with a number of strategic "corrections" and changes, directly into the Koran.

Through the years, such doctrinal borrowing has proliferated as pious Moslem scholars have attempted to discern the sundry palimpsests that led to the corruption of faith through the centuries—thus finding the essential core of Islamic truth in all religions. The Sunnis—the largest branch of Islam and the one that Egyptian president Hosni Mubarak subscribes to—adopted the pietism and oligarchism from the Platonists. The Shiites—the branch of Islam that Hashemi Rafsanjani of Iran subscribes to—adopted occultation and channeling from the Cabbalists. The Sufis—the branch of Islam that Saddam Hussein subscribes to—adopted antinomianism and dualism from the Zoroastrians. The Alawites—the branch of Islam that Hafez al Assad of Syria subscribes to—adopted reincarnation and thetanism from the Hindus. The Takfirs—the branch of Islam Kuwait's Emir Jaber al Ahmed subscribes to—adopted positivism and materialism from the Nestorians. And the Wahhabis—the branch of Islam that King Fahd of Saudi Arabia subscribes to—adopted pragmatism and determinism from the Monophysites.

Despite this modicum of eclecticism, Islam has remained remarkably untainted by lax moral or doctrinal standards. By and large it is conservatively puritanical. Instead of being shaped by these outside influences, it has subsumed them into its universal hegemony and extended its legacy by baptizing them by proxy.

The second ambition of Islam that enables it to claim the legacy of ancient empires for itself is *Ji'had,* holy war, or *al Harb.* According to Islamic tradition, the complete military subjugation of the earth is mandated by Allah. The conquests of the Moslems' Babylonian, Assyrian, and Persian forbearers thus provide a living paradigm for their present task.

In the *Hadith,* Mohammed said:

> Hear, O *Muslims,* the meaning of life. Shall I not tell you of the peak of the matter, its pillar, and its topmost part? The peak of the matter is Islam itself. The pillar is ritual *Rakatin* prayer. And the topmost part is *Ji'had*—holy war.[8]

The Medinese *Suras* likewise encouraged all the faithful to take up the sword or the martyr's robe with civil and social enforcement:

> The *Umma* who stay at home—apart from those who suffer from a grave impediment—are not equal to those who fight for the cause of Allah with their goods and their persons. Allah has given to those who fight a higher rank. He has promised all a good reward; but far richer is the recompense of all who fight against the infidel for him.[9]

The *Suras* go on to assure the believers that Allah is with them and will honor their sacrifice:

> Prophet, rouse the faithful to arms. If there are twenty steadfast men among you, they shall vanquish two hundred; and if there are a hundred, they shall rout a thousand of the infidels, for they are devoid of understanding.[10]

Jews and Christians are specifically singled out as the primary targets of this *Ji'had:*

> Fight against such of those to whom the Scriptures were given as believe not in Allah. They must be utterly subdued for they worship their rabbis and their monks as gods.[11]

The great success of the empires of the ancient Middle East provides encouragement and impetus for Moslems to faithfully carry out the command to wage holy war. The weight of glory is great. Islam thus needs the foundational support of the distant past. And so, the legacy of Babylon, Assyria, and Persia, as incongruous as it may seem, is happily embraced in the name and the spirit of Allah.

The Lessons of History

At the State Department in Washington, talk of strategic initiatives or troop movements or diplomatic maneuvers is likely to attract keen interest. On the other hand, talk of the spiritual and historical forces that invigorates those strategic initiatives or motivates those troop movements or dominates those diplomatic maneuvers is likely to cause eyes to glaze over.

Thus, it is not only the militant affinity of modern Islam with the primordial spiritual ambition of Babylon, Assyria, and Persia that underlies the crisis in the Middle East; it is also the inability, and perhaps even the refusal, of the West to *deal* with that militant affinity.

If we continue to ignore the spiritual dimensions of this conflict, we will be wrecked upon the shoals of history just as surely as Babylon, Assyria, and Persia once were. It is an ancient script now unfolding in the Middle East:

> Do you have eyes but fail to see, and ears but fail to hear? And don't you remember? (Mark 8:18)

CHAPTER FOUR

EAST OF HIS BROTHERS: ISHMAEL AND ISAAC

The power struggle between Israel and the Arabs is a long-term historical trial. Victory or defeat are for us questions of existence or annihilation, the outcome of an irreconcilable hatred.

Al Riyadh Saud

Ishmael will be a wild donkey of a man, his hand will be against everyone, and everyone's hand will be against him, and he will live to the east of his brothers.

Genesis 16:11–12

As the *muezzin* began the haunting call to prayer on the morning of October 8, 1990, some three thousand of the faithful gathered in front of the El Aqsa Mosque on *Haram es Sherif*, Jerusalem's famed Temple Mount. But instead of quietly making their way into the mosque, the *Umma*, the true believers of Islam, began to stockpile rocks, bricks, bottles, scraps of iron, and other makeshift weapons.

Forty feet below, nearly twenty thousand Jewish pilgrims and tourists, entirely oblivious to the disaster brewing up on the Mount, were celebrating *Succot* at the Wailing Wall.

Suddenly cries of *Allah Akbar*, Allah is great, *Ji'had*, holy war, and *Itbakh al Yahud*, slaughter the Jews, erupted over the mosque's loudspeakers. A well-orchestrated assault then began. The stockpiled weapons were hurled down upon the heads of the Jewish worshipers. A small police outpost on the Mount was burned to the ground. Huge boulders were rolled across nearby intersections to prevent police reinforcements from entering the area. And an unruly mob of teenagers began ransacking the shops and stores in adjacent neighborhoods.

The melee lasted for nearly an hour. About forty Israeli policemen tried to disperse the rioters with tear gas and rubber bullets, but to no avail. The enraged Moslems fought back with axes and chains. Rocks continued to rain down from the Mount. The streets of the Old City were rife with rioters.

Finally, the police resorted to live ammunition. When the dust cleared, twenty-one Moslems lay dead; and the crisis in the Middle East had just escalated out of control. The world was on the verge of war in the Persian Gulf; and now, suddenly, there was another front: Israel.

Another cheerless chapter was about to be written in the eternal blood feud between Ishmael and Isaac.

The Doubt of Abraham

Abraham was known as a man of faith. But it is the fruit of his doubt that has most shaped the spiritual and geo-political crisis in the Middle East today.

God promised him an heir. When he came up out of Ur in the land of the Chaldees, God told him that through that heir, the nations would be blessed. Through that heir a mighty people would be raised up that would be the focal point of faith, hope, and love the world over. Abraham believed, and thus became the "friend of God."

But that promised heir was not forthcoming. Years passed, then decades. As the time slowly wore on, Abraham began to have subtle doubts. He began to fear that he had perhaps misunderstood God's promise. Sarah, his wife, was barren; and they both were becoming quite elderly. The possibility of a natural heir seemed increasingly impossible. So he and Sarah decided to take matters into their own hands.

In some parts of the ancient Middle East, it was obligatory for a barren wife to provide her husband with an indentured concubine who would bear children for her by proxy. Legally, the children were to be the issue of the wife, not the servant. In their doubt, Abraham and Sarah resorted to this surrogacy scheme; and a child was thus conceived. They named him Ishmael.

Fourteen years later, they saw how foolish they had been ever to doubt God's promise. A child was born to Sarah at the age of ninety. The natural heir they had yearned for was theirs. They named him Isaac.

Conflict between these two sons of Abraham began almost from the start. One was "born according to the flesh" and the other was "born according to the spirit" (Galatians 4:29). The one, disinherited by the other, apparently became bitter, "mocking" and "persecuting" his half brother. Eventually, the situation became so intolerable that Sarah demanded that Ishmael and his Egyptian concubine mother Hagar be expelled from the family to wander in the desert (see Genesis 21:9–21).

Sadly, that was not the end of the matter. It was only the beginning.

According to the Bible, Ishmael went to live in the wilderness of Paran, in the region of Hejaz (see Genesis 25:18). There he had twelve patriarchal sons, as did both of his nephews, Jacob and Esau. Scripture associates the clans and tribes descended from him with the Midianites, the Edomites, the Egyptians, and the Assyrians (see Genesis 37:36, 28:9, 39:6, 25:18). Interestingly, this concurs with Islamic tradition, which asserts that Ishmael settled in the city of Mecca, which eventually became the capital of Hejaz and the holy city of Islam. There he became the unquestioned leader of all the diverse desert peoples throughout the Middle East.

Meanwhile, Isaac begat a long line of faithful men—
Jacob, Joseph, Moses, Joshua, Gideon, and David—who
were able to claim the full inheritance of Abraham: the
land of Israel.

Thus, from Isaac came the Jews.

From Ishmael came the Arabs.

And the two have been at enmity with one another ever
since.

The First Palestinian Conflict

Israel is the Promised Land of the Jews (see Genesis 12:7).
It is their Abrahamic inheritance (see Genesis 15:18–21).
But throughout history they have inhabited it only rarely.

When Moses secured freedom from slavery in Egypt for
his people, he led them back to that patriarchal homeland.
They had been absent four hundred years. During that
time, others had inhabited the region. The Canaanites,
Ammonites, Edomites, Moabites, Midianites, and Philistines
had made their homes in and around Palestine and were
hardly inclined to recognize Israel's prior claim. In addition, the original settlers—the Kenites, the Kenizzites, the
Kadmonites, the Hittites, the Perrizites, the Rephaim, the
Girgishites, and the Jebusites—were equally uncooperative.
War between Ishmael and Isaac was inevitable.

According to the Bible, the conquest of the land under
the leadership of heroes of faith and valor like Joshua,
Caleb, Othniel, Ehud, Shamgar, Deborah, Gideon,
Jephthah, Samson, Samuel, Saul, and David was a long,
bloody, and torturous affair not to be forgotten by either
side. Ever.

The *Sahih Moslem* annals written during the time of
Mohammed's *Hijra* in Medina assert that:

> The criminal Jews have brought destruction upon the
> *Umma* since the earliest times. Their leaders conspired to
> send the innocent of Canaan away from their homes.
> They repulsed the pleas of the Philistine widows and

Moabite orphans and washed their fields in the blood of the Ammonite poor. Therefore, they shall not stand in the day of judgment, nor shall they prevail against the sure coming of *Ji'had*. Allah shall pronounce just retribution and the *Umma* shall observe with joy and gladness.[1]

Egyptian President Anwar Sadat, before he signed the extraordinary Camp David Accord with Israel, said:

The assassination of Arab brethren, like Goliath, by Jewish sheep-herders like David, is the sort of shameful ignomy that we must yet set aright in the domain of the occupied Palestinian homeland.[2]

And Yasser Arafat declared:

Be assured that the many indignities heaped upon the Palestinian people since ancient times must and shall be avenged. Israel's policy in the occupied territories is little more than an extension of the imperialist tactics of the conqueror Joshua. Surely the judgment of Allah is reserved for them until Palestine is transferred from *Dar al Harb* to *Dar al Islam*. Ishmael shall have his revenge.[3]

Following the demise of the kingdoms of Israel and Judah at the hands of the Assyrians and Babylonians, it seemed that indeed Ishmael had his revenge. But then the Persians restored Isaac to Palestine, and the ancient rivalry was resumed, beginning with Tobiah and Sanballat's challenge of Ezra and Nehemiah.

The advent of Greek and Roman imperial rule quelled the fires of hatred for a time. Stability was forcibly imposed on the Middle East by the legions of the West until the Roman armies laid waste to Palestine, crushing the aspirations of both Ishmael and Isaac.

Suddenly, they were back to square one.

The Second Palestinian Conflict

Most of the Jews who survived the destruction of Jerusalem and the devastation of the land at the hands of the Romans in A.D. 70 joined the already large *diaspora* in exile. But a few continued to try to scratch out a living in the blighted environs of Palestine.

During the period of Roman—and later Byzantine— rule, Palestine was utterly neglected. Its poverty became abject. The once lush gardens and fertile fields were left to the scourge of the harsh elements. Trees and vegetation were cut away with profligate indulgence. What little remained of the once beautiful architecture deteriorated badly due to neglect. Even so, the Jews were legally protected and thus could work and worship in relative peace and security. And because the entire Arab population had converted to Christianity, Palestine simply became a tiny Jewish island in the vast sea of the Christian Middle East.

But then came Islam.

During the time that he was exiled from Mecca, Mohammed launched a fierce *Ji'had* against the significant Jewish communities of Hejaz. In Medina, the interim headquarters of his nascent movement, he had the Jewish men scourged and decapitated in the public square. He then divided their women, children, animals, and property among his followers.

During this time he recorded in his Koranic revelations the immutability of the eternal conflict between Moslems and Jews:

> You shall surely find the most violent of all men in enmity against the *Umma* to be the Jews (5:82).

> O, true believers, take not the Jews and Christians for your friends. They cannot be trusted. They are defiled— filth (5:51).

> The Jews are smitten with vileness and misery and drew on themselves indignation from Allah (2:61).

> Wherever they are found, the Jews reek of destruction— which is their just reward (3:112).

According to the Meccan chronicles of that early period, recorded in the *Sahih Moslem* annals, all Jews were anathema and were to be annihilated:

> Allah's messenger—may peace be upon him—has commanded: Fight against the Jews and kill them. Pursue them until even a stone would say: Come here Moslem, there is a Jew hiding himself behind me. Kill him. Kill him quickly.

For the first time in centuries, the old feud between Ishmael and Isaac had been revived.

As he gained more and more control over the Arabian peninsula and then over the entire Mediterranean world, Mohammed tempered his policy of wholesale slaughter. Expediency dictated that much. Many of the hated Jews proved to be valuable assets to his administration. Some had professional skills and resources. Others had economic skills and resources. Thus, he began to find it politic to invent a kind of treaty, or *Dhimma,* merely to subjugate his beaten foes, sparing their lives in exchange for a tithe of half of their property, to be levied in perpetuity. Christians and even Jews were thus spared, as long as they continued to contribute to the ongoing support of *Ji'had* with the substance of their wealth.

Eventually, *Dhimma* became more sophisticated. The subject peoples were given the right to live and to practice their religion on a limited basis. They even received protection in return for payment of special taxes: the *Kharaj,* or land tax; the *Ji'zya,* or poll tax; the *Fadlak,* or travel tax; and the *Sult'ah,* or special taxes levied at the ruler's pleasure. The problem was that the status of the captive people was always at risk, since the *Dhimma* merely suspended the conqueror's Koranic right to kill them and confiscate their property. Thus, it could be revoked at even the slightest whim.

Mohammed died in A.D. 632. But the scourge of *Ji'had* and *Dhimma* had only begun. Over the next decade, Mohammed's successors, Caliph Abu Bakr and Caliph

Umar, were able to consolidate their military control over all of Arabia, from the Hejaz to Najd and from Asir to al Hasa. They conquered most of Sassanid Iraq and Byzantine Egypt. They made serious advances against Syria that permanently destabilized that important Christian province. And by 638, they had conquered Palestine as well.

Thousands of Jews were slaughtered along with the Byzantine Christians. A few of the most technically proficient Jews continued to live under the Moslem domination of *Dhimma*—Baghdad, Kairouan, and Ummayid Spain all boasted strong Jewish professional communities—but most of the rest fled into uneasy exile in Christian Europe. In any case, Palestine was emptied of its indigenous population once again, and the conflict between Ishmael and Isaac was made moot. Again. But only for a little while.

The Third Palestinian Conflict

Zionism was born in Europe among well-educated Jewish professionals who had finally come to realize that absorption into western culture was utterly impossible. It seemed to them that the path to acceptance was hopelessly blocked by either prejudice or avarice, or perhaps even worldview incompatibility.

After centuries of persecution, hardship, humiliation, pogroms, ghettoes, and purges, the nineteenth century had brought them to the place of almost universal emancipation. But even with official legal restrictions removed, the unofficial cultural animus of anti-Semitism in Europe continued to wield overwhelming force.

The Jews began to dream once again about the possibility of returning home from their long-imposed *diaspora*. They began to dream once again of Zion.

The Zionist ideal was, of course, not entirely new. For nearly two millennia, wherever there was a community of Jews, some yearned for a return to Erez Israel. And ambitious European politicians and monarchs often proposed a resettled Jewish state in Palestine as a possible solution to various difficulties both at home and in the decrepit Middle East. But with the writings of Moses Hess, Emmanuel Deutsch, Benjamin Disraeli, Emma Lazarus, and George Elliot a whole new notion was conceived: a secular Jewish state.

And then came Theodor Herzl.

Herzl was a journalist for the liberal Vienna daily, *Neue Freie Presse.* While covering the shameful trial of Alfred Dreyfus, a French army officer wrongly accused of treason and mercilessly vilified on racial grounds, he experienced a dramatic conversion of the soul. He became an ardent Zionist. Zionism became his driving passion. He lived it and breathed it. Within months he transformed what had been little more than wishful thinking for centuries into a political movement. His book, *Der Judenstaat,* became the lightning rod for two generations of Jews who had struggled, fought, bled, and died to realize their ambition.

Inspired by Herzl's vision and supported by a world-wide network of Zionist organizations, Jewish families began to return to Palestine, buying up small tracts of barren desert and abandoned ruins from the doddering Ottoman overseers. After World War I, when the British assumed responsibility for the administration of the region, first a small trickle and then a steady stream of Jewish settlers made their way out of the lands of persecution back to Zion. After World War II, when the horrors of the Holocaust were revealed to the world, a literal flood of exiles returned from the *diaspora.*

For the first time in centuries, Ishmael and Isaac lived in proximity to one another. And not surprisingly, tensions flared almost immediately.

The British tried desperately to appease both sides. The Balfour Declaration in 1917 committed the government to supporting the Zionist cause, but concerns for the indigenous Arab population caused them to recalcitrantly waffle. A bitter cycle of demonstrations, strikes, riots, terrorism, and reprisals followed—on both sides of the conflict—for

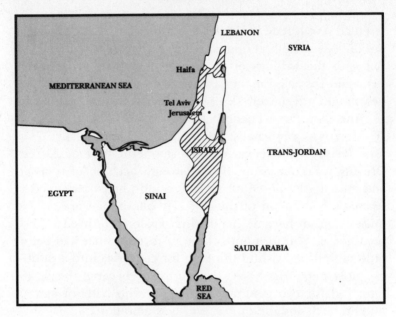

1947 U.N. PARTITION PLAN

more than three decades. In frustration, the British together with the newly constituted United Nations, partitioned the district of Palestine. They designated the western fourth as a Jewish Palestinian state and the eastern three fourths as an Arab Palestinian state and gave the two new nations autonomy. Their intention was to settle the question once and for all. Their intention was to bring peace to the region. Their intention was to give the people of both Trans-Jordan, as the new Arab state was called, and Israel, as the new Jewish state was called, freedom, security, and self-determination.

All those intentions were good. But of course, even the road to hell is paved with good intentions.

The day after Israel officially became a nation on May 14, 1948, three Palestinian Arab armies—the Najada Forces, the Arab Liberation Army, and the Futuwa Defense, League along with the national military forces of Lebanon,

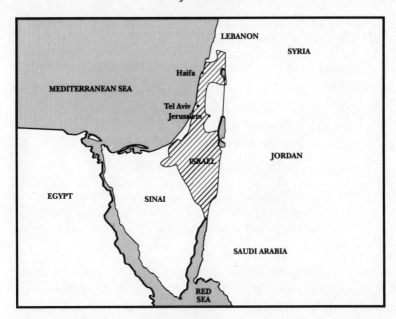

1948 LINES OF FURTHEST ISRAELI ADVANCE

Syria, Egypt, Jordan, Iraq, and several contingents from the Saudi Arabian Army—launched a bitter war for control of the entire Palestinian region.

According to the Arab leaders, there was absolutely no possibility for any sort of compromise or negotiated peace.

Haj Amin el Husseini, the *Mufti* of Jerusalem who had served the Nazis during World War II and who now led the Palestinian Arab resistance, declared:

> The entire Jewish population in Palestine must be destroyed or be driven into the sea. Allah has bestowed upon us the rare privilege of finishing what Hitler only began. Let the *Ji'had* begin. Murder the Jews. Murder them all.[4]

King Abdul Aziz Ibn Saud, the founding monarch of the Saudi sultante, said:

> The Arab nations should sacrifice up to ten million of their fifty million people, if necessary, to wipe out Israel.

Israel to the Arab world is like a cancer to the human body. And the only way of remedy is to uproot it.[5]

Azzam Pasha, secretary general of the Arab League, asserted that:

This will be a war of extermination and a momentous massacre which will be spoken of like the Mongolian massacres and the Crusades. No Jew will be left alive.[6]

King Farouk of Egypt concurred:

The Jews in Palestine must be exterminated. There can be no other option for those of us who revere the name of Allah. There will be no *Dhimma*. There will only be *Ji'had*.[7]

From King Abdullah of Trans-Jordan to Zahir Shah of Afghanistan, from Imam Yahya of Yemen to King Hassan of Morocco, from Reza Shah of Iran to Regent Abd al Ilah of Iraq, every Moslem leader in the Middle East called for the destruction of Israel and the execution of the Jews. Even the moderate King Idris of Libya sounded the call for genocide:

The Zionist conquest of Palestine is an affront to all Moslems. This colonialist barbarism cannot and will not be tolerated. There can be no compromise until every Jew is dead and gone.[8]

Israeli leaders responded tenaciously that they would fight to the death to keep and defend their new land holdings, and they swore that one day they would occupy Jerusalem as well.

Although the war ended in a stalemate—with Israel keeping most of the territory it was allotted in the partition plus some—the animosity between Ishmael and Isaac only intensified. Successive wars in 1956, 1967, and 1973 made their conflict a global concern. In addition, the terrorist strikes of the Palestine Liberation Organization (PLO) and the protracted involvement of Israel in the Lebanese civil

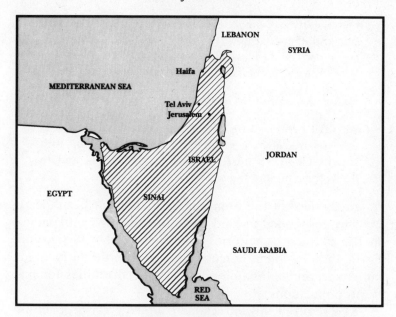

1967 POST SIX-DAY WAR FRONTIERS

war served only to aggravate the open wounds of dispossession, anarchy, and geo-political strife. Violence and strife have become a regular part of the Palestinian landscape—as familiar as the Judean hills.

And still, the hatred is unabated.

Sheikh Tamimi, the current *Mufti* of Jerusalem who was responsible for organizing the ill-fated Temple Mount uprising, recently issued a call for all Moslems to join arms against Israel at a time when it seemed that the Persian Gulf crisis might permanently disrupt Islamic unity:

> The Jews are destined to be persecuted, humiliated, and tortured forever, and it is a Moslem duty to see to it that they reap their due. No petty arguments must be allowed to divide us. Where Hitler failed we must succeed.[9]

Yasser Arafat, the longtime chairman of the PLO and the mastermind behind the *Intifada* uprising in the West Bank and Gaza Strip, has said again and again:

Our objective is simply the liberation of the Palestinian soil and the establishment of a Palestinian state over every part of it. Thus, the Jews must be removed and Israel must be annihilated. We can accept nothing less.[10]

Hafez al Assad of Syria agreed:

We shall never call for nor accept peace. We shall only accept war. We have resolved to drench this land with Israel's blood, to oust the Jews as aggressors, and to throw them all into the sea.[11]

In the face of this animosity, a number of Israeli leaders have responded in kind by authorizing new settlements in the occupied territories won from Jordan, Syria, and Egypt, limiting the movement and civil liberties of Palestinian Arabs, and inhibiting economic opportunities for minority populations.

As a result of this intractable conflict, every problem in the Middle East is now somehow connected to the Palestinian question. For instance, when Saddam Hussein overran Kuwait in 1990, he blamed the conflict on Israel. Likewise, when Hafez al Assad completed his conquest of Lebanon that same year, he blamed the crisis on Israel. When Muammar Qaddafi of Libya sparked a coup in Chad, also in 1990, he blamed the situation on Israel. This seemingly absurd linkage has become inescapable.

As Hashemi Rafsanjani of Iran explained:

Every problem in our region can be traced to this single dilemma: the occupation of *Dar al Islam* by Jewish infidels or Western imperialists. Every political controversy, every boundary dispute, and every internal conflict is spawned by the inability of the *Umma* to faithfully and successfully wage *Ji'had*. The everlasting struggle between Ishmael and Isaac cannot cease until one or the other is utterly vanquished.[12]

And so the conflict continues. The blood of Abraham continues to be spilled with prodigal abandon.

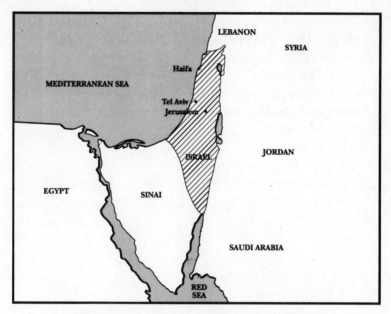

1967 POST CAMP DAVID ACCORD

The Lessons of History

The conflict between the Jews and the Moslems is not a question of borders or settlements or political self-determination. Thus, it cannot be be solved simply by manipulating the political apparatus. It is an intractable spiritual problem. And it must, therefore, be dealt with in spiritual terms:

> Though we walk in the flesh, we do not war according to the flesh. For the weapons of our warfare are not carnal but mighty in God for pulling down strongholds, casting down arguments and every high thing that exalts itself against the knowledge of God, bringing every thought into captivity to the obedience of Christ. (2 Corinthians 10:3–5, NKJV)

To approach the crisis in the Middle East in any other fashion is to invite disaster. That, of course, is not to say that we are to "become so heavenly-minded that we are of no earthly good." It is to say however, that we cannot deal with a problem effectively if we treat only the symptoms and ignore the root causes.

And the root causes in the Middle East are first and foremost spiritual, not military.

CHAPTER FIVE

JI'HAD: THE UNENDING WAR OF CONQUEST

We shall never call for or accept a negotiated peace. We shall only accept war—Ji'had—the holy war. We have resolved to drench the lands of Palestine and Arabia with the blood of the infidels or to accept martyrdom for the glory of Allah.

Abdul Aziz Ibn Saud

Though we walk in the flesh we do not wage war in the same manner as that of the world.

2 Corinthians 10:3

O n the morning of November 4, 1979, in the holy city of Qom, the patriarch of the Shiite faith—the man many Moslems believed to be either the long-awaited *Caliph* of all Islam or perhaps even the prophesied incarnation of the occulted *Mahdi*—was seething with righteous indignation. Allah's revolution of righteousness was in danger, he told his small audience of *Mullahs, Imams,* and students. The enemies of Islam were attempting to undermine the liberation of the *Umma.* The Great Satan was at large right in their midst. Something must be done, he said as he dismissed them. The "nest of spies and infidels" must be eliminated.

Word spread quickly. Ayatollah Ruhollah Khomeini had spoken.

Within a few hours, the small demonstration of young people that regularly gathered outside the American embassy on Taleghani Street in Teheran, some eighty miles north of the Ayatollah's humble residence, had grown into a swarming mob. Before noon, they had burst into the compound chanting, "Death to America!" "Death to the Infidels!" "Death to the Great Satan!" *"Ji'had! Ji'had! Ji'had!"*

The embassy personnel and their marine guards secured themselves in the chancellery building to wait for the Iranian police or perhaps even the army to restore order. But they never came. By early afternoon the mob had taken the frightened Americans hostage.

But the full dimensions of the drama had yet to be revealed.

Early the next morning Seyyed Khomeini, the Ayatollah's son, visited the embassy and conferred with the militant captors. In a hastily called press conference at the gate of the compound he told the milling masses that he, like his father, supported the takeover.

Meanwhile, America looked on in horror and disbelief. Disturbing television footage of the hostages, bound and gagged and paraded about like game after a hunt, were beamed into millions of living rooms. Images of madcap street demonstrations of flailing, shouting, and cursing Moslem fanatics were etched on the nation's conscience. It was a nightmare come to life. Madness seemed to have overtaken the world.

The *Ji'had* had begun. Again.

The Infidels

During the formative years of his faith, Mohammed had very little contact with Christianity. He may have heard the stories from Christian merchants and caravaneers who passed through the Hejaz on their way across the Arabian peninsula from time to time. But those occasions were few and far between.

That limited exposure contrasted sharply with his contact with Judaism. During his *Hijra,* or exile to Medina, he apparently had a series of acrimonious experiences with the Jewish community there. As a result, while the Koran hurls bitter invectives at the Jews, its condemnation of Christianity is rather mild.

Mohammed revered Jesus as "one of the prophets" (2:135). It was only a misunderstanding on the part of Christ's disciples, he contended, that led them to worship Him as the Son of God. They were therefore to receive special consideration as "people of the book" (29:46).

Even so, they were still infidels (2:140) and had to be dealt with as such. That meant that they were, unwittingly or not, guilty of shameful idolatry (6:20–23). They were thus subject to the judgment of God (22:17). And they were subject to the wrath of the *Umma*—the true community of Islam (9:4).

In other words, Christians were a legitimate target for the *Ji'had,* the holy war. Like the Jews, they were either to be subjugated and brought under *Dhimma,* or they were to be killed. No other option was tolerable to the faithful Moslem:

> Who will protect them, by night or by day, from the Lord of Justice? Yet they are unmindful of their Lord's remembrance. Have they any other means to protect them? Their idolatry will be powerless for their salvation. Nor shall they be protected from our scourge. Good things have been bestowed upon these men and upon their fathers. They have lived long and prospered. But now, we shall invade their lands and curtail their borders. Can they then triumph? They have been warned by inspiration, but the deaf can hear nothing. (21:41–46)

The *Ji'had* was therefore to be pursued at all costs. Death was of no concern to the Moslem because, according to the Koran, those who died at the hands of the infidels during the *Ji'had* were actually martyrs, earning a certain and immediate entrance into paradise (3:156–59). In fact, martyrdom was considered to be the devotional pinnacle of *al Salaam,* or Islamic submission (3:167–75).

During the first four decades of the seventh century, Moslem armies began to engage the defenses of the Christian Middle East. With the divine assurance of ultimate victory and the comfort of devotional martyrdom inspiring them, it is not surprising that the Moslem troops threw themselves into battle with passion, vision, and potency. And it is not surprising that, more often than not, they won.

Byzantium

At that time, the far-flung Byzantine Empire had become a manifest monument to the beneficence of Christian culture. Throughout the Middle East, across North Africa, and deep into the heart of Europe, imperial stability and steadfastness had spawned a remarkable flowering of culture.

The legal system was just and efficient. Government was limited and decentralized. Trade was free and prosperous. Families were stable and secure. Perversity and corruption were suppressed while personal liberty and civil rights were enhanced. Advancement in the sciences was unprecedented. Art, music, and ideas flourished as in no other time in human history. And the literary output was bedazzling.

One visitor to the capital, Fulcher of Chartres, expressed complete awe at its vast achievements:

> How splendid a civilization, how stately, how fair, how spiritually inclined, how many palaces raised by sheer labor in its highways and streets, how many works of art, marvelous to behold. It would be wearisome to tell of the abundance of all good things; of gold and silver, of charity and grace, of garments of varied appearance, and of sacredness unimaginable.[1]

Another visitor at the time, Maedock of Alliers, marveled at the general happiness of the Byzantine culture:

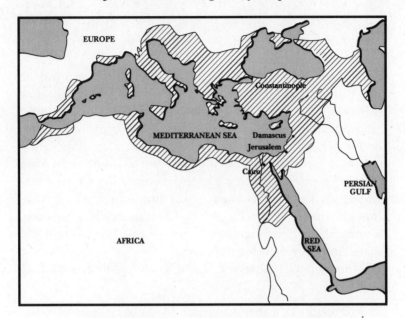

EUROPE

Constantinople

MEDITERRANEAN SEA Damascus
Jerusalem

Cairo

PERSIAN GULF

AFRICA

RED SEA

BYZANTINE EMPIRE 560 A.D.

The evident misery in so many other domains is seemingly altogether absent here in the East. The prosperity and liberty enjoyed by all has had a melodious effect upon them. Industry and labor is undertaken with gladness of heart. Benediction is upon every tongue. Surely God's grace has rested upon them.[2]

The Byzantine church was quite robust as well. Evangelistic missionary endeavors had spread the gospel message from Scandinavia to China and from the depths of Africa to the steppes of Russia. Theological orthodoxy was insured by regular creedal councils, canonical synods, and conciliar presbyteries that decentralized authority and power among several episcopacies and patriarchates. And local congregational vitality was catalyzed by an emphasis on strong preaching and a sacramental parish life.

Despite all these apparent strengths, the foundations for Byzantine unity had a number of hidden weaknesses.

Most significantly, the long-lived stability of the imperial order had encouraged a lax estimation of the importance of military preparedness.

When the Islamic armies first began to venture out of the Arabian desert, they quickly saw and exploited that weakness. Though often greatly outnumbered by the huge and well-equipped Byzantine forces, the fearless tenacity of the Moslems enabled them to prevail time after time. They swarmed almost suicidally onto the battlefield in vast human waves. Their valor was unreserved, their fervor untempered. Their malevolence was unrelenting, their passion unbridled. They fought not for themselves or their homelands or their ideology or their race. They fought for Allah. And they died for paradise.

One imperial observer, Lameh Chrysostine, stated at the time:

> It is almost as if they are driven by the very demons of Hell itself. They are in no wise tempted by comfort or safety. Instead, I dare say, they relish the ardor of battle and welcome the horrors of death.[3]

The caliph Umar—who led those early stinging campaigns along the southern frontier of Syria, into the fertile Mesopotamian valley of Iraq, along the Nile in Egypt, and ultimately into Palestine itself—was a stern giant of a man with a long dark beard and a full, brooding countenance. He wore coarse, frayed garments and always carried a whip in his right fist in order to enforce righteous humility among his men. He had little appreciation for the accomplishments of Byzantium and was singleminded in his desire to bring the empire to its knees.

According to the *Shah Nemeh*, a contemporary chronicle of caliphs and kings, Umar despised the Christian infidels for their "half-faith" and yearned to force their confessions, creeds, and liturgies into extinction:

> Umar—may he ever have peace—coveted nothing in the flesh save the undoing of Christian arrogance; for Jews

are impotent and pagans are powerless; but in Christians he saw challenge. Therefore, his meat was their humiliation; his drink was their shame; his humor was their downfall; his very breathing was their destruction. To see the whole earth bow in submission to Allah was his sure desire; but to see Christendom fall was his great delight.[4]

Clearly, Umar pursued that delight with great vigor and proficiency. By A.D. 634, his armies had completed their conquest of Syria. By 635 he controlled much of Egypt. And by 636, he had defeated the Byzantines decisively in the great battle of Yarmuk, thus attaining unchallenged authority throughout the Fertile Crescent.

But Umar was not content.

In February 638, he entered Jerusalem riding on a white camel. As always, he was dressed in his worn, filthy robes; and the army that followed him was rough and unkempt. But its discipline was perfect and its victory complete. The cardinal city of Christendom with all its shrines, relics, monasteries, and holy places was now in the hands of Islam.

And still Umar was not content.

Before his death in 644, he had spread the dominion of Islam from the Euphrates across the North African Littoral. He had conquered all of Iraq, brought the Persians to the brink of collapse, controlled the southern Mediterranean coastline, and put Christendom on the defensive at every turn. In addition, he left his successors a tumultuous momentum that gave them expansive new conquests in Spain, Sicily, Crete, and Italy.

It was not until 733, when Charles Martel stopped the Moslem advance north of the Pyrenees, that this first great period of Islamic expansion came to an end. In just one hundred years time, the map of the venerable old Mediterranean world had practically been transformed from one vast Christian empire into a vast Islamic one.

Though the *Ji'had* had failed to conquer the entire world, it had come torturously close.

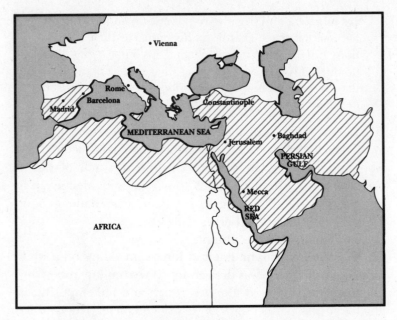

THE ADVANCE OF ISLAM 900 A.D.

The Crusades

The loss of Christian Egypt, Syria, and Iraq sent shudders of fear throughout the kingdoms of the West. The penetration of Moslem armies into Spain, France, and Italy shook their confidence even more. And the vulnerability of Byzantium was utterly terrifying. But it was the occupation of the Holy Land, Jerusalem, and Palestine, that most disturbed them. Ultimately, it was only the desecration of the sacred sites of the Christian faith that spurred them into concerted and forthright action.

At the Council of Clermont in 1095, Pope Urban II issued a call that was heard throughout Europe:

> From the confines of Jerusalem and from the city of Constantinople a horrible tale has gone forth. An accursed race, a race utterly alienated from God, has invaded the lands of those Christians and depopulated them by the sword, plundering, and fire.[5]

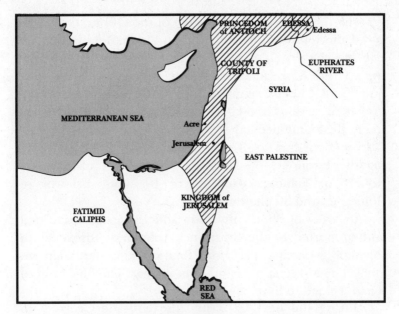

CRUSADER KINGDOMS 1100 A.D.

He went on to list in detail the atrocities of the Moslems: the desecration of churches, the rape of Christian women, the torture of priests and monks, the pilfering of villages and towns, and the occupation of the territories.

He appealed to both their sense of Christian mercy and their sense of national honor:

> Recall the greatness of Charlemagne. O most valiant soldiers, descendants of invincible ancestors, be not degenerate. Let all hatred between you depart, all quarrels end, all wars cease. Start upon the road to the Holy Sepulcher, to tear that land from a wicked race and subject it to yourselves thereby restoring it to Christ. I call you to take the cross and redeem defiled Jerusalem.[6]

Immediately, a stirring chant arose from the crowd there at Clermont: *Deus Vult,* God wills it. It was a chant that would quickly spread throughout Europe.

The following year, the Crusades began in earnest.

The lure of booty, the mystery of the Orient, the promise of the remission of penance, and a chaste sense of justice and chivalry all played their part amongst the intoxicating mixture of spiritual and fleshly motives which drew the knights of Christian Europe into battle with Islam. Whatever their reasons, the knights and nobles that would eventually hear and heed the call of the pope were the best Christendom had to offer. They included Robert of Normandy, Raymond of Toulouse, Bohemond of Taranto, Robert of Flanders, Godfrey of Bouillon, Baldwin of Boulogne, and Stephen of Blois.

An army of about fifty thousand Europeans, outfitted and supported by the Byzantines, relentlessly drove south through Syria and Palestine, finally taking Jerusalem in 1099. The Moslems at last were in retreat. The bludgeon of *Ji'had* seemed to have been broken.

During the next few years, the Crusaders carved up their conquests into several kingdoms and duchys. They built castles, churches, and markets. They constructed fortified walls, dug fresh wells, and cultivated the fields. They restored the holy places. They opened the trade routes. And they rebuilt the roadways.

Many of the men committed the rest of their lives to making the region a flourishing Christian culture once again. But there simply were not enough of them to hold their tiny strip of territory against the onslaught of the Moslems.

In 1144, the Moslems reorganized their armies and swept through Syria. Edessa fell. A second crusade led by the kings of France and Germany failed to recover it. All of Europe was stunned. And the worst was yet to come.

In 1150, Saladin united the Islamic world under his leadership and began to chip away at the remaining Christian holdings. In 1187, he defeated the Crusaders at the decisive Battle of Hattin. He then captured Jerusalem and overran virtually all the Latin territories except Acre.

A series of new Crusades led by notables such as King Richard the Lion-Hearted of England, Emperor Frederick II of Germany, and King Louis IX won back a few swatches of the lost lands but were generally ineffectual. Jerusalem was lost for the last time in 1244, and Acre finally fell in 1291. And although the Crusader movement continued its efforts until 1798, when Napoleon seized the last Templar stronghold on Malta, the only successes it had were outside the Middle East—in Southern France against the Albigensians, in Spain against the Moors, and in Austria against the Saracens.

Attack and counter-attack seemed to be over. For a little while, at least.

The Tides of Time

Because *Ji'had* is an innate aspect of Islam, the ambition to conquer the world and subjugate the infidels has never been abandoned by the Moslems. From time to time they experience revival and launch a new initiative. The rise of the Ottoman Empire in the fifteenth and sixteenth centuries very nearly succeeded where Umar and Saladin ultimately failed.

The Ottomans were the descendants of savage Saljuk Turk tribesmen from the Mongol steppes. Their conversion to Islam in the eleventh century was followed with an unrivaled zeal for *Ji'had*. By the beginning of the twelfth century they had gained control of the Anatolian Plateau and were challenging the old Byzantine strongholds of Asia Minor.

Decades passed, then centuries. The Ottomans only grew in strength while their rivals all slowly atrophied. First the Caliphate fell into their hands. Finally, control of all of Islam was theirs. And then, in 1453, they apprehended the greatest prize of all: Constantinople fell. The Byzantine Empire came to an end after more than a millennium.

When the news reached Europe, there was panic in the streets. Economic fortunes were lost overnight. Political careers were destroyed, and whole theologies were suddenly cast into bankruptcy. The greatest symbol of Christian culture—and Europe's link to the mysteries of the East—had been overrun by the heathen.

Doomsayers had a heyday. They predicted catastrophe and destruction. Experts on Bible prophecy began to expound new theories about a coming Great Tribulation and a terrible Apocalypse. Talk of the Last Days and the End Times occupied the attention of Christians everywhere. Complex formulas were contrived to prove that the Antichrist and False Prophet had come and that the Great Whore of Babylon had been revealed. Charts were drawn up to show the increasing frequency and intensity of earthquakes, famines, and plagues. The Signs of the Times seemed to indicate that the countdown to Armageddon had actually begun.

While the Europeans occupied themselves with hysterical speculative eschatology, the Ottomans expanded their conquests. Sultan Selim called for a renewed *Ji'had* and added Greece, Macedonia, and the Balkans to his empire. His son, Suleiman, swept into Belgrade in 1521, expelled the Templars from Rhodes in 1522, and conquered Hungary in 1526. Then in 1529 he entered the very heart of Christian Europe, ready to crush the church once and for all. According to one of his chroniclers at the time, he confidently boasted:

> The infidels will at last bow in submission to Allah. The time for judgment has come just as their prophets have said. The *Ji'had* has advanced its full course and the end is now in sight. The abomination of the Christian heresy shall be no more.[7]

His seige of Vienna that winter was in a very real sense Europe's last stand. If he had prevailed there, no army of any significance would have been able to stop him until he reached

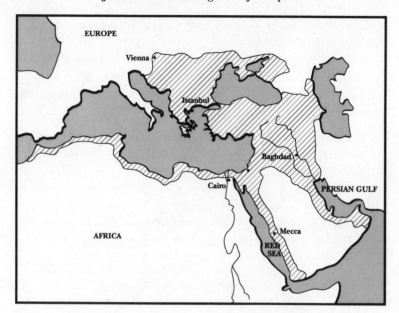

THE OTTOMAN EMPIRE 1530 A.D.

the outskirts of Paris. But because of a valiant and united defense, he did not prevail, and Christendom was saved.

After Suleiman passed from the scene, calls for *Ji'had* came only sporadically—during times of Islamic revival or at revolutionary flashpoints. The Ottoman Empire drifted into a mediocre stasis. And the West began to forget about its Eastern nemesis while it rushed headlong into cosmopolitan modernity.

The resurgence of Arab nationalistic fervor that followed World War II in Egypt and Syria under the leadership of Gamal Abdel Nasser was a short-lived attempt to reestablish the hegemony of Saladin or Suleiman on a secular foundation. But its momentum simply could not outlast the charismatic leader who first gave it impetus. When he died, it died.

And then came the Ayatollah Khomeini and the frightening specter of his Islamic Fundamentalism—which was really nothing more than a return to historic and orthodox Koranic Islam.

His sudden overthrow of the Shah in Iran in 1979 renewed the international call for *Ji'had*. Shortly after installing his revolutionary government in Teheran, the Ayatollah asserted:

> We shall export our revolution to the whole world. Until the cry *"Allah Akbar"* resounds over the whole world, there will be struggle. There will be *Ji'had*.[8]

He continued:

> Islam is the religion of militant individuals who are committed to truth and justice. It is the religion of those who desire freedom and independence. It is the school of those who struggle against imperialism. Weapons in our hands are used to realize divine and Islamic aspirations. The more people who die for our cause, the stronger our *Ji'had* shall become.[9]

His plea was explicit: faithful Moslems were to wreak havoc the world over in the name of Allah. Western nations were to be overthrown. Any option open and available should be exercised for the sake of Islam, from terrorism to revolution, from subversion to full-scale war:

> The governments of the world should know that Islam cannot be defeated. Islam will be victorious in all the countries of the world, and Islam and the teachings of the Koran will prevail all over the world.[10]

Therefore, he continued:

> We have in reality, then, no choice but to destroy those systems of government that are corrupt in themselves and also entail the corruption of others, and to overthrow all treacherous, corrupt, oppressive, and criminal regimes. This is the duty that all Moslems must fulfill, in every one of the Moslem countries first, and then throughout the infidel West, in order to achieve the triumph of our revolution and to garner the blessing of Allah.[11]

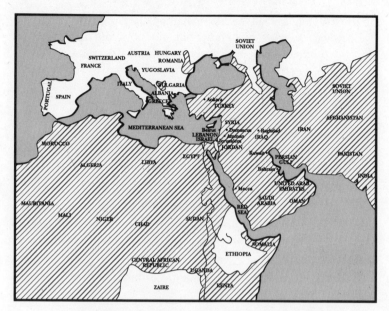

THE WORLD OF ISLAM 1991 A.D.

There would be—in fact, there could be—no compromise. The die was cast. The stage was set.

The recent spate of terrorism—highjackings, bombings, kidnappings, attacks, and even direct military confrontations—that has been inflicted upon the West is clear testimony to the fact that Islam's *Ji'had* is anything but a forgotten relic of the past.

The Lessons of History

During the days of mobilization for World War I, when it looked for a time that American troops would be deployed in the Middle East against the fierce Ottomans, a young Presbyterian pastor, James Alexander Bryan, eloquently expressed the key message of the ages:

> Let all be done in bathed prayer—our working and our playing, our eating and our sleeping, our dreaming and

our doing. Let all be done bathed in prayer. But most
particularly, when we know that our boys, our sons, and
our brothers, and our husbands, must face those deni-
zens of terror from the desert realms of the Levant,
should we bathe our very inner being, our breathing,
and our thinking in prayer. Dost thou not know that the
hosts of Cain and the minions of Babel, the legions of
Saracene and the hordes of Arabia are set from eternity
against the covenant people. Pray therefore. Night and
day, pray. Moment by moment, pray. Pray for mercy. O
dear souls, pray.[12]

Pray, because the passion for *Ji'had* will not go away
simply because we deploy troops in impressive and deadly
array. Pray, because the desire for *Dhimmi* will continue to
divide East and West despite our carefully constructed international coalitions and strategic alliances. Pray, because
it's never over 'til it's over.[13]

CHAPTER SIX

LOOSE ENDS: THE PEACE TO END ALL PEACE

The true Umma—the community of Islam—fight in the way of Allah; all infidels in the way of idols. So true Moslem, fight the friends of Satan. Then in the day of peace there will come a sudden overturning and the oppressors will come to nought.

Koran 4:78; 26:228

When they say, "Peace and safety!" then sudden destruction comes upon them, as labor pains on the pregnant woman. And they shall not escape.

1 Thessalonians 5:3

At one time, Beirut was known the world over as the jewel of the Mediterranean. With its spectacular beaches, its splendid hotels, and its moderate climate, it had become the playground of the jet set and the most desirable destination in the entire Middle East. But those days are now long gone. Beirut is little more than a bombed-out shell. It is a trash-strewn, rubble-filled, grief-stricken battlefield where the acrimonious ambitions of the region have overtaken its everyday life and brought to ruin its civilization.

In 1983, President Ronald Reagan sent a large contingent of crack American troops, including an entire Marine

75

battalion, to that war-torn city as part of the United Nations' Multinational Peacekeeping Force. He hoped their presence would help bring an end to the bitter civil war that had divided Lebanon's Christian and Moslem populations since at least 1975.

On the morning of October 23, a large cargo truck loaded with explosives made its way into Beirut's international airport toward the Marine command center. As the suicide bomber crashed his truck into the building, he was heard screaming his final message to the world: *"Allah Akbar! Ji'had! Ji'had! Ji'had!"* Moments later, rescuers began frantically digging through the rubble of twisted steel and crumpled concrete searching for survivors. Instead, they found 241 Americans dead and scores more crippled for life. In an anonymous telephone call after the attack, a group calling itself the Islamic *Ji'had* claimed responsibility for the attack and promised many more to come.

Less than six months later, the president gave up his hopes for peace in the region and ordered the remaining troops home.

They returned gladly.

Because the Middle East has been the battleground for men's passions since the beginning of time, virtually every scheme imaginable has been attempted in the hope that one day real and lasting peace might be attained. Invariably, whenever the West has assumed the role of peacemaker, either conquest, colonialism, containment, or appeasement has been at the heart of its scheme.

And just as invariably, such mechanistic and materialistic methodologies fall short of the mark of peace.

Conquest

In 1796, a young Corsican military commander for the French republic made a name for himself in a series of innovative land maneuvers that liberated all of Lombardy from the dominion of Austria. Well educated, properly connected, and insanely ambitious, Napoleon Bonaparte effulgently guided his motley legions against the infinitely larger and better equipped armies of the Habsburgs, the Hohenzollerns, the Wettins, the Wittelsbachs, and the Oldenburgs. He swept aside their superiority in battle after battle with unconventional ripostes and ambushes. His achievements were nothing short of brilliant.

But it seems his ego was at least as great as his achievements were. By the time he had established republican rule in Venice, Milan, and Genoa, he had already begun to imagine himself an imperial conqueror. He styled himself a Caesar.

He returned to Paris a hero. The city, weary and worn from the long traumas of revolutionary anarchy, was anxious for some beacon of hope. From the people in the streets to the nobles in the salons, Napoleon represented that hope. He was successful. He was undefeatable. And he was irrepressible.

So confident was the government in his abilities that the Directorate urged him in 1797 to assume leadership of all the French armed forces and lead an expedition, first to pacify England, and then to pacify the world.

Thinking more like a Roman Caesar or a Greek Alexander than a modern European general, he redirected their focus:

> The key to containing the English and to bringing peace to the world is not to attack England. It is to capture the Levant and control all its commerce with India and the East. Peace has always turned upon Alexandria, Jerusalem, Acre, and Constantinople. It always will. Control them and you can control the world. Bring them peace and you bring peace to the world.[1]

And so the French Caesar set out to wage his peace.

Eluding the English fleet in the Mediterranean, his forces crossed from Malta to the mouth of the Nile and quickly occupied the great old city of Alexandria. The mea-

ger Turkish defenses surrendered. Shortly thereafter,
Aboukir and Cairo also capitulated. Although his naval support was no match for the English flotilla, he confidently
moved out from under its cover and on to Jaffa and Acre.

His plan was to secure Egypt, Syria, Palestine, and ultimately the entire Middle East, as a platform to launch a
series of worldwide conquests. It was to be the first prize in
a far-flung French empire—the beginning of a glorious
new *Pax Française.*

But all did not work out as planned.

First, Admiral Nelson captured the vulnerable French
fleet in the Aboukir Bay, cutting Napoleon off from reinforcements and supplies. Then, the Turkish defenders at
Acre retreated into the old Crusader battlements where
they could not be flushed out. Finally, ethnic and tribal
disputes nullified any advantage that he might have gained
from the diplomatic alliance that he had forged with indigenous Arab sultanates.

In 1799, Napoleon gave up and fled the region. Despite
the fact that he had the overwhelming advantage over his
foes—he had by far the finest fighting force, the most brilliant strategy, and the clearest vision—he was soundly defeated. His dream of peace in the region eluded him.

Of course, Napoleon would quickly recover from that
first defeat and rise to unimagined heights. But he would
never forget his difficult foray into peacemaking-by-con-
quest in the Middle East. He wrote from St. Helena at the
end of his life:

> Of all the defeats that I have tasted none has been so
> bitter—not even Waterloo—than my defeat at Acre. For
> it was there that Fate or Providence determined that I
> should never rule the world and that a French-directed
> peace would never prevail. I knew it then. I knew it ever
> afterward. No empire can ever be wrought without the
> peace of Jerusalem at its center because that is the hinge
> of history. But then, no empire can ever be wrought with
> the peace of Jerusalem at its center because such peace

is humanly unattainable. It is an impossible mysterious mistress.[2]

Napoleon had to learn the lesson that would-be conquerors have been learning in the Middle East for centuries: sheer force or superior armaments or finely hewn strategies are simply not sufficient to bring peace to the region. It is a wild and unpredictable land where swirling spiritual obsessions and disparate human passions compete on an even keel with steadfast reason and cold pragmatism.

Napoleon had to learn that the hard way.

Colonialism

The accession of the Christian culture of Europe as the world's dominating socio-political force was actually not assured until well into the nineteenth century. In fact, for the bulk of its first two millennia Christian culture had been strikingly unsuccessful in spreading its deleterious effects beyond European shores. In the Far East, missionary endeavors were practically non-existent in China and paralyzed by persecution in Japan. In India, the higher castes were virtually untouched by the gospel, and even the lower castes showed only transitory interest. South America's conversion to the conquistadors' Catholicism was tenuous at best. And tropical Africa had proven to be so formidable and inhospitable that western settlements were confined to a few small outposts along the coast. Ever since the Middle East had been lost to Islam, Christianity had become little more than a regional phenomenon.

There had been, of course, a few bursts of expansion beginning in the sixteenth century. Explorers began to tentatively venture out into uncharted realms. Scientists began to probe long-hidden mysteries. Traders and merchants carved out new routes, new markets, and new technologies. Energies that had previously been devoted exclusively to survival were redirected by local magistrates into projects and programs designed to improve health, hygiene, and the common good. Africa, India, China, Indonesia, and the Americas were opened to exploration and exploitation. From colonial outposts there, a tremendous wealth of exotic raw resources poured into European cities.

Despite all these advantages, however, European advances were limited and short-lived. Internecine warfare and petty territorialism disrupted, and very nearly nullified, even that much Christian influence. From 1688 (when William and Mary concluded the Glorious Revolution in England by ascending to the throne, Louis XIV canonized the iron-fisted notion of divine right, and young Peter Romanov became czar of all the Russias until 1848—when the calamitous Marxist rebellions in Paris, Rome, Venice, Berlin, Parma, Vienna, and Milan were finally squelched) Europe was racked by one convulsive struggle after another.

But then, almost suddenly, everything changed.

Three great revolutions beginning first in England and then spreading throughout all the European dominions laid the foundations for this turn of events.

The first was the Agricultural Revolution. The replacement of fallowing with leguminous rotation, the use of chemical fertilizers, and the introduction of farm machinery enabled Europeans to virtually break the cycle of famine and triage across the continent for the first time in mankind's history.

The second was the Industrial Revolution. Manufactured goods and the division of labor created a broad-based middle class and freed the unlanded masses—again, for the first time in human history.

The third was the Transportation Revolution. At the beginning of the nineteenth century, Napoleon could not cross his domain any more efficiently than Nebuchadnezzar could have six centuries before Christ. By the end of the Victorian age, men were racing across the rails and roads in motorized vehicles of stupendous power, crashing over and under the waves of the sea in iron vessels of enormous size, and cutting through the clouds in ingenious zeppelins, balloons, and planes.

Within a single generation, the earth became a European planet. Whole continents were carved up between competing monarchs. Africa, Asia, Australia, the Far East, Latin America, and even the Middle East became the backyard playgrounds of speculative colonialists and imperial opportunists.

England differed from its rivals in that it had somehow come to realize that peace could not be won by naked conquest alone. It attempted to exact peace through colonization. The beach-head for the British in foreign lands was trade, not war. Instead of sending armies, they sent merchants. Not surprisingly, the merchants were less threatening than the armies and were more often than not very well received. As a result, the empire of Queen Victoria grew at a phenomenal rate and became mind-bogglingly prosperous. In Africa, India, and the Far East, English businessmen established an economic commonwealth that only gradually became a full-fledged political empire.

In the Middle East, that same kind of colonial philanthropy enabled Britain to step into the void left by the dismantled Ottoman Empire after World War I. But it was in for a rude awakening.

Unprepared for the roiling passions that divided various Moslem factions, the bitter acrimony between the Jews and their neighbors, and the pitiful rivalry of innumerable tribal and ethnic legions, the English peacemakers found themselves on the horns of an awful dilemma. For several decades they tried to extricate themselves from what their diplomats called The Eastern Question—all to no avail:

- In 1916, they concluded the Sikes-Picot negotiations with France, thus denying the possibility of Arab hegemony.

- In 1917, they issued the Balfour Declaration, pledging to secure the establishment of a Jewish Palestinian state.

- The next year, they accepted and endorsed Woodrow Wilson's Fourteen Points as a basis for a cessation of hostilities in World War I, including the guarantee of autonomy for the Arabs as a precondition for the armistice.

- In 1919, they embraced the Hashemite Emir Faisal's Plan for Arab National Unity presented to the Supreme Council at the Paris Peace Conference.

- In 1920, they accepted the National Pact presented by the Ottoman Chamber of Deputies, thus permanently dividing the old Syrian districts.

- In 1921, they offered the Hashemite, Abdullah, free sovereignty in Trans-Jordan and exemption from the Balfour Declaration.

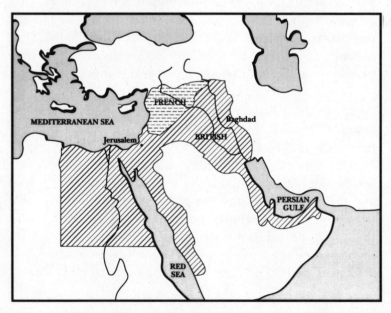

EUROPEAN DOMAINS 1918 A.D.

- In 1922, they released a statement of British Policy on Palestine, responding to both Arab and Zionist pressures by establishing the Hashemite regencies in Iraq, Hejaz, Syria, and Palestine.

- In 1925, they approved the ouster of the Hashemite, Sharif Hussein from Mecca, and the subsequent absorbtion of Hejaz into the Saudi Kingdom.

- In 1928, they finalized a treaty with Trans-Jordan and Iraq, enraging the Zionists due to its betrayal of the conditions of Balfour.

- In 1937, they severely restricted Jewish immigration to Palestine with the Ridenour Policy, thus stranding hundreds of dispossessed souls on the island of Cyprus.

- And in 1946, they attempted to partition Palestine into Arab and Jewish regions—a plan endorsed by the United Nations and partially implemented in 1948.

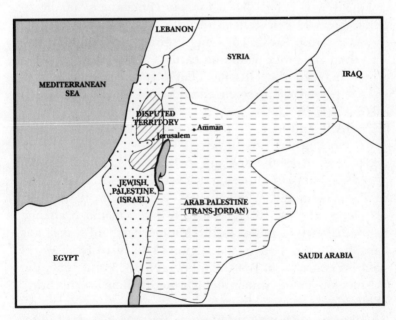

THE PARTITIONING OF PALESTINE 1948 A.D.

The problem with these painfully negotiated policies, concords, treaties, pacts, alliances, and settlements was that virtually every one of them contradicted all the others. The colonizing principle that seemed to work so well in other parts of the world, ushering in an age of *Pax Britannia,* failed miserably in the complex and discrepant Middle East.

Finally, in frustration, the British peacemakers pulled out in 1948. Their only other foray into the region ended in disaster in 1956 at the Suez Canal.

Like Napoleon, they had to learn the hard way.

Containment

Ever since the imperial armies had secured the southern territories along the Black Sea in 1558, the Romanov Czars that successively ruled the vast dominions of Russia coveted a warm water port—a trade outlet to the Mediterranean. In addition, they believed that a forcible containment of the Islamic threat to their strategic security, was absolutely crucial.

As a result, Russia has fought more wars in the Middle East than any other nation on earth.

It engaged the Ottoman Turks seven different times over a period of three hundred years—in 1568–1869, in 1678–1881, in 1697–1700, in 1710–1711, in 1736–39, in 1828–1829, and in 1877–1878. It engaged Persia four times over a period of two hundred years—in 1722–1723, in 1804–1813, in 1906–1909, and in 1911–1912. And it has engaged Afghanistan three times over a period of one hundred years—in 1885–1886, in 1941–1943, and in 1979–1989.

None of those struggles ever resulted in much change in the balance of power in the Middle East and Russia was continually rebuffed in the region. The rest of the world paid little attention. But then, between 1853 and 1856, the Russian policy of containment brought them to the brink of world war in the Crimea.

In a jurisdictional dispute over the holy places of Ottoman-controlled Jerusalem, Czar Nicholas I finally determined to protect and enforce the interests of Christians within the Turkish Empire's territories. The Ottoman emissaries in Russia were outraged at the Czar's audacity and spurned all his attempts to communicate directly with the Sultan. In frustration, Nicholas ordered his forces to occupy Turkish Moldavia, Serbia, and Wallachia. The Ottomans quickly declared war.

Fearful of Russian intentions, France, Britain, Austria, Sardinia, and Prussia all signed defensive pacts with the Turks. In addition, thousands of Bedouins and Arab merchants volunteered to beat the Russian "infidels" away from their borders. A short time later, when a Russian naval squadron bombarded and destroyed an Ottoman flotilla at Sinop, the new international alliance of Europeans and Arabs moved into the area, and launched a bloody and protracted war. After the battle of Balaklava—immortalized in Tennyson's famous poem *The Charge of the Light Brigade*—Russian troops were forced into retreat and the Czar was compelled to sue for peace.

Like the French and the British, he failed to recognize the conflux of spiritual passions and geopolitical jealousies that make containment—or any other mere material policy—in the Middle East utterly hopeless.

Appeasement

The past hundred years have been dubbed "The American Century" by modern historians, and for good reason. America's transformation from a provincial and isolated republican experiment in the nineteenth century to an international superpower in the twentieth is one of the most stunning events in human memory.

Like the French, the British, and the Russians, Americans have sought to wield their influence around the globe in order to encourage freedom and to establish peace. But they have done it while repudiating conquest, colonialism and containment. Rather than trying to occupy or balkanize regions, the United States has sought merely to influence. It has sought to leverage competing concerns and balance intractable conflicts. It has taken the course of appeasement.

At first blush, the strategy appeared to be a good one: use the leverage of foreign aid and strategic cooperation to win friends and influence enemies, to stymie the advances of the Soviet Union, and to open new markets for American products and investment.

Practically, though, the result of this kind of foreign policy, particularly in the Middle East, has produced scant improvement over our Western predecessors. It has often led us to fund both sides of a conflict—building simultaneously the Israeli and the Arab military capabilities—on the pretense that a balance of power serves as the best hedge against Communism. It has often led us to betray our proven friends and support our sworn enemies—allowing the *Phalangist* and *Maronite* Christians under the leadership of General Aoun to be massacred by Hafiz al Assad's *Hisbollah* Syrian troops in Lebanon—on the pretense that stability in the region required the sacrifice of certain interests. And it has led us to befriend despots and defend tyrannies—allying ourselves with Saudi Arabia and Kuwait, where slavery and indentured servitude are still practiced—on the pretense that international pluralism must make room for cultural diversity.

Far from securing American interests and concerns, this kind of philosophical and moral schizophrenia has led us into one dead end after another.

Consider the remarkable record of American appeasement with Saddam Hussein and Iraq:

- When Iraqi Exocet missiles killed thirty-seven United States seamen aboard the *Stark* in 1987, the State Department blamed Iran and excused our ally Hussein altogether.

- When Iraq used chemical weapons in a genocidal attack on its own Kurdish citizens in 1988, our government turned a blind eye.

- Even after Hussein established Baghdad as a haven for international terrorists—including Abul Abass, the hijacker of the *Achille Lauro*—we removed Iraq from our list of terrorist states.

- In 1989, the Bush Administration refused to join twelve other western nations calling for a United Nations inquiry into Iraqi human rights violations.

- In 1990, our government also failed to protest the forcible relocation of more than half a million Kurds and Syrians in Iraq.

- The Administration successfully fought against the legislative efforts of Senators Jesse Helms, Caliborne Pell, and Al d'Amato to impose sanctions on Iraq and its suppliers.

- Since 1982, we have provided Iraq with more than five billion dollars worth of American products and taxpayer-guaranteed loans and subsidies.

- We have also in recent years secured for Hussein nearly three hundred million dollars of credit from the Export-Import Bank.

- Days before the invasion of his Persian Gulf neighbor, the United States Ambassador to Iraq told Hussein that, since we had no defensive alliances with Kuwait, we saw the conflict between the two nations as a routine Arab border dispute.

- Though Iraq had invaded Kuwait twice previously and was threatening to do so again—voicing the same grievances each time: in 1961, 1973, and 1990—our government deigned to remain neutral.

- On the very day before the invasion of Kuwait, Bush Administration officials were on Capitol Hill lobbying for an increased financial aid package for Iraq.

- Yet, one week later, Saddam Hussein was labeled as a Hitler and a madman who simply had to be stopped.

Like Napoleon's conquests, Britain's colonization, and Russia's containment, America's appeasement has failed to bring peace to the region. Because all three approached the Middle East from a mechanistic and materialistic perspective—assuming that the imposition of Western notions of pluralism, economic development, and international cooperation are paramount values shared by all—they failed miserably to comprehend the complex maze of spiritual and historical factors that catalyzes the crisis in the Middle East.

We too have had to learn that lesson the hard way.

True Peace

The prophet Isaiah brought a message to those who lived in the Middle East thousands of years ago. Amazingly, that message is as relevant today as when he first uttered it:

> Let there be peace—peace to him who is far off and to him who is nearby. I will bring healing to the land of the righteous. But as for the wicked, they are like the tossing sea. It cannot be quiet, and its waters toss up refuse and mud. Therefore, there is no peace for the wicked. (Isaiah 57:19–21)

With remarkable economy and startling clarity, that message traverses both space and time to bring into focus the complex dilemma of bringing peace to our strife-riven world.

Throughout his life, Isaiah had dedicated himself to proclaiming God's eternal purposes for mankind. He was a diligent bearer of the glad tidings of peace. After all, God had established a covenant of peace with His people (see Isaiah 54:10). It was an irrevocable and everlasting covenant (see Isaiah 61:8). Thus, they had the promise of peace with the nations around them and with God Himself (see Isaiah 26:12; 27:5). They would have "peace like a river"

(Isaiah 66:12) and "peace like the waves of the sea" (Isaiah 48:18). It would be a perfect peace wrought by the Prince of Peace (see Isaiah 26:3; 9:6).

This remarkable promise of peace was indeed good news and glad tidings. But Isaiah made it abundantly apparent that the promise could be redeemed only by the righteous. "Peace on earth and good will toward men" is available only to those "on whom God's favor rests" (Luke 2:14). No peace, much less this promised utopian peace, will ever be attained by use of sheer force or aggression. No peace will ever be attained by mere appeasement or compromise. No peace will ever be attained by clever negotiation or wily manipulation. Nothing could be clearer: "There is no peace for the wicked" (Isaiah 48:22). There never has been and there never will be.

The Lessons of History

Things just aren't always as they seem. That is the dilemma of living in a fallen world. G. K. Chesterton brilliantly captured the essence of this dilemma when he wrote:

> The real trouble with this world of ours is not that it is an unreasonable world, nor even that it is a reasonable one. The commonest kind of trouble is that it is nearly reasonable, but not quite. Life is not an illogicality; yet it is a trap for logicians. It looks just a little more mathematical and regular than it is; its exactitude is obvious, but its inexactitude is hidden; its wildness lies in wait . . . It is this silent swerving from accuracy by an inch that is the uncanny element in everything. It seems a sort of secret treason in the universe. An apple or an orange is round enough to get itself called round, and yet is not round after all. The earth itself is shaped like an orange in order to lure some simple astronomer into calling it a globe. A blade of grass is called after a blade of the sword, because it comes to a point; but it doesn't. Every-

where in things there is this element of the quiet and incalculable.[3]

Mirroring the world's fallenness, the uncanny element in the efforts of the West to achieve peace in the Middle East is its silent swerving from accuracy by an inch. Its exactitude is obvious, but its inexactitude is hidden; its wildness lies in wait. It is almost operatic in its unreality, creating a peace to end all peace.

Things just aren't always as they seem.

Even so, God has called us to peace (see 1 Corinthians 7:15). He has called us to be peacemakers (see Matthew 5:9). If we genuinely desire a true peace, a lasting peace, and a just peace, then we have only one course to follow—the course of righteousness. Therefore, "Let us pursue the things that make for peace" (Romans 14:19).

PART THREE

THE FUTURE
AND FAITH

Nothing is more unbecoming than sullenly to gnaw the bit with which we are bridled, and to withhold our groaning from God, if indeed we have any faith in His promise.

John Calvin

I charge you before God and the Lord Jesus Christ, who will judge the living and the dead at His appearing and His kingdom: preach the Word. Be ready in season and out of season. Convince, rebuke, exhort, with all longsuffering and teaching. For the time will come when they will not endure sound doctrine, but according to their own desires, because they have itching ears, they will heap up for themselves teachers; and they will turn their ears away from the truth, and be turned aside to fables.

2 Timothy 4:1–4

CHAPTER SEVEN

BACK TO BABEL: THE
NEW WORLD ORDER

What we demand is nothing peculiar to ourselves. It is that the world be made fit and safe to live in, and particularly that it be made safe for every peace-loving nation which, like our own, wishes to live its own life, determine its own institutions, be assured of justice and fair dealing by the other peoples of the world as against force and selfish aggression. For our own part, we see very clearly that unless justice be done to others it will not be done to us. The program of the world's peace, therefore, is our program.

Woodrow Wilson

Come let us build ourselves a City and a Tower whose top reaches the Heavens; let us make a Name for ourselves, lest we be scattered abroad to the uttermost parts of the earth.

Genesis 11:4

He is perhaps the best credentialed man ever to sit in the Oval Office. His background and personal achievements are stunning. After graduating from Yale he had an heroic tour of duty in the armed forces, ran a successful business, was active in community life, and was keenly involved in local party politics. From his earliest days at the university he made the right connections, did the right things, joined the right organizations—from the Skull and Bones Club to the Trilateral Commission and from the Republican party to the Episcopal church. His distinguished public service career has sent him to Washington as a congressman, to China as an ambassador, to New York as the American envoy to the United Nations, and then back to Washington first as the director of the Central Intelligence Agency, and then as vice president.

Not at all unlike one of Plato's philosopher kings, George Herbert Walker Bush has developed a very unique vision of the world as a result of the very unique experiences life has afforded him. It is a vision of peace, justice, harmony, and unity. It is a vision of reason, cooperation, compassion, and prosperity. It is a vision of nothing less than a New World Order.

And now, as president of the United States—arguably the most powerful and influential man on the face of the earth—he would implement that vision and usher in a bright and fortuitous New Age. Speaking before a joint session of Congress, he said:

> The crisis in the Persian Gulf, as grave as it is, also offers a rare opportunity to move toward an historic period of cooperation. Out of these troubled times a New World Order can emerge.[1]

President Bush is not the first gifted, powerful, and munificent ruler to be driven by the vision of a New World Order or a New Age. In fact, that vision is as ancient as man himself.

The Tower of Power

According to the Bible, the first concerted effort to establish a New World Order came at Babel:

> Now the whole earth was of one lip and had but one language. And it came to pass, as they journeyed eastward, that they found a plain in the land of Shinar, and they dwelt there. Then they said to one another, "Come let us make bricks and bake them thoroughly." They had brick for stone and mud for mortar. And they

said, "Come, let us build ourselves a city, and a tower whose top will reach into the heavens; let us make a name for ourselves, lest we be scattered abroad over the face of the whole earth." (Genesis 11:1–4)

Apparently, the goal of Nimrod and the other members of this seventy-nation alliance (see Genesis 10:2–32) was to establish the global enforcement of at least five major objectives:

First, they desired to preserve some sort of universal cultural consensus, or world-wide ideological communion, among the nations. The Biblical account asserts that the "the whole earth was of one lip and had but one language" (Genesis 11:1). The word *Saphah*, translated *lip* here, literally means "creed" or "confession." It wasn't just that all of the nations spoke the same language. It was that they spoke the same language because they were bound by the same culture. They were of one mind. They shared a common philosophical outlook. They had the same worldview. Babel, then, was simply an attempt to institutionalize that unity so that it might be adequately preserved.

Second, the leaders of the international coalition at Babel wanted to impose increasing secularization on human society. According to the narrative, these events occurred as the nations journeyed east (see Genesis 11:2). Throughout the Bible, eastward migrations are invariably associated with rebellion against the will and purposes of God. The word *Nasa*, translated *journeyed* here, literally means to "pull out," or "abandon." When Adam and Eve abandoned Eden, they journeyed east (see Genesis 3:24). After Cain killed his brother Abel, he abandoned his home and journeyed east (see Genesis 4:16). When Lot abandoned Abram to seek his fortunes in the lush valley of Sodom, he journeyed east (see Genesis 13:11). Again and again the pattern is reinforced in Scripture: moving east is symbolic of abandoning righteousness. Babel, then, was a very straightforward rebellion against God's standards of morality and ethics in society.

Third, the organizers of the Babel debacle wanted to secure their base of power. The Biblical account says that they set to work building "a tower whose top will reach into the heavens" (Genesis 11:4). Of course, they knew that they could not build an architectural structure that would pierce the atmosphere and intrude into the heavenly realm. A tower in the ancient world was a kind of artificial mountain sanctuary where men could grasp the power of the divine. The Garden of Eden was on a mountain (see Ezekiel 28:13–14). But ever since the Fall, when men were denied access to that sanctuary, they had sought appropriate alternatives since they were not satisfied with the alternative that God Himself had provided (see Genesis 3:16-26). Having been barred from the presence of God, they aspired to literally storm the gates of His habitation by building a kind of "stairway to heaven." They were trying to "steal holy fire." They were trying to secure the blessing, and perhaps even the power, of God on their own terms and by their own strength. Babel was simply a humanistic power play. It was a ploy designed to "end run" God's providence.

Fourth, the perpetrators of the Babel incident sought to establish their autonomy and self-determination. The narrative says that they wanted to "make a name" for themselves (Genesis 11:4). Throughout the Bible, naming is a very significant activity. A person's name defined his character. If a person's character altered significantly sometime during his life, his name would be altered as well. Thus, whenever anyone was converted, his name was changed. For instance, Abram was changed to Abraham, Sarai to Sarah, Jacob to Israel, Simon to Peter, and Saul to Paul. In every case, it was either a parent or God Himself who did the naming. But the leaders of the seventy-nation alliance at Babel determined that they would short-circuit that divine prerogative and make a name for themselves. Babel, then, was a declaration of independence from God. It was an act of prideful, humanistic rebellion.

Fifth, the pioneers of the New World Order at Babel attempted to centralize control over every aspect of the social structure. The Genesis account says that they were fearful of being "scattered abroad over the face of the whole earth" (Genesis 11:4). The only reason they were frightened of that was that God had told them to scatter. They were frightened of obedience to His will:

> Be fruitful and multiply; fill the earth and subdue it; have dominion over the fish of the sea, over the birds of the air, and over every living thing that moves upon the earth. (Genesis 1:28)

> Be fruitful and multiply, and fill the earth. And the fear of you and the dread of you shall be on every beast of the earth, on every bird of the air, on all that move on the earth, and on all the fish of the sea. They are given into your hand. (Genesis 9:1–2)

Once again, the purpose of Babel was to subvert God's sovereign purposes for human society by institutionalizing an alternative, centralized authority structure: their own.

Though the effort was rather ingenious, the great experiment on the plain of Shinar failed miserably—as all attempts to mechanically establish a New World Order eventually do:

> But the Lord came down to see the city and the tower which the sons of men had built. And the Lord said, "Indeed the people have become one and they are of one lip, and this is what they begin to do; nothing that they propose to do will be withheld from them. Come let Us go down and there confuse their lip, that they may not be able to understand one another's language." So the Lord scattered them abroad from there over the face of all the earth, and they stopped building the city. Therefore its name is called Babel, because there the Lord confused the lip of all the earth; and from there the

Lord scattered them abroad over the face of all the
earth. (Genesis 11:5–9)

The alliance was broken. The universal creed was confused. The tower was deserted. And the New World Order
was thrown into disarray. For a time.

The Empire Impulse

G. K. Chesterton warned that we should always:

> Beware of men and of movements that speak the lan-
> guage of Babel. Regardless of whether they are Commu-
> nists or Fascists, Universalists or Deists, Socialists or Capi-
> talists, Alchemists or Templars, Liberals or Conservatives:
> beware of their New World Order; beware of their Peace
> In Our Time; beware of their New Age; beware of their
> Fraternal Harmony; beware of their *Novus Ordo
> Saeculorum*. It is merely part and parcel of that same
> Tower of Babel impulse which God cursed so long ago. It
> is merely a new sprig from the primordial root of hu-
> manism: man seizing his own destiny and making a
> name for himself in the annals of history.[2]

Sadly, just as the attraction of empire building has always plagued mankind, the language of Babel continues to
be the common currency of modern diplomacy. In fact,
virtually all of the most influential voices in the international community are of one lip and of one language. They
all cry out for the global establishment of the principles of
Babel—hegemony, secularism, power, autonomy, and centralization—over and above any other concerns. The empire impulse is still very much alive.

The United Nations, for instance, was founded in 1945
as "man's last hope for peace." But its interest in peace has
been terribly selective through the years. Instead, it has
steadfastly lobbied for the principles of Babel. When the
Soviet Union invaded Hungary in 1956, Czechoslovakia in
1968, and Afghanistan in 1979, the United Nations Security

Council uttered nary a peep. Somehow, it also overlooked the blandishments of genocide in Cambodia in 1975, the stench of triage in Ethiopia in 1984, and the legions of international terrorism in Libya in 1986. When hundreds of Christian Maronites were captured, bound, lined up, and slaughtered in the streets of Lebanon in 1990 by the Syrian army, the United Nations did not even take notice. After all, Syria had become a "partner for peace" in the Middle East and a "strategic ally" in making the United Nations' New World Order a reality.

Anything and everything, anyone and everyone, is expendable for the sake of Babel. The goal of achieving real peace is continually subverted to serve other ends—the ends of globalism and internationalism. As historian Paul Johnson asserted, before President Bush gave it an infusion of new life in 1990:

> The United Nations had become a corrupt and demoralizing body, and its ill-considered actions were more inclined to promote violence than to prevent it.[3]

Because the United Nations had been so fitfully jockeying for the New World Order and One World Government, it simply did not have time to play the pipes of peace. Because it was so busy establishing and subsidizing the various organs of international centralization—the World Economic Community, the World Health Organization, the World Food and Energy Council, the World Bank, the World Council of Interdependence, and the World Affairs Council—it has simply ignored the globe's hottest hot spots. Because virtually every powerful internationalist institution—the Council on Foreign Relations, the Trilateral Commission, the Royal Institute for International Affairs, the Skull and Bones Club, and the Aspen Institute—recognizes the United Nations as the perfect forum for the implementation of their disparate Babel objectives, genuine peace has been shunted off the agenda.

When the crisis in the Middle East was inflamed once again by Iraq's invasion of Kuwait, the advocates of the New World Order saw an opportunity to realize their designs at long last. President Bush asserted:

> We are now in sight of a United Nations that performs as envisioned by its founders.[4]

That is indeed an ominous prospect. We would do well to heed the warning of Jesus:

> Which of you, intending to build a tower, does not sit down first and count the cost, whether he has enough to finish it—lest after he has laid the foundation, and is not able to finish it, all who see it begin to mock him, saying, "This man began to build and was not able to finish." Or what king, going to make war against another king, does not sit down first and consider whether he is able with ten thousand to meet him who comes against him with twenty thousand? Or else, while the other is still a great way off, he sends a delegation and asks conditions of peace. (Luke 14:28-32, NKJV)

The End Times

There are many who fear that the road to a New World Order is not only fraught with danger, it is quite literally the road to ruin as well. They believe that the chronology of recent events in the Middle East is a countdown to Armageddon. They assert that the current crisis is pregnant with eschatological importance.

There are many others who see little if any prophetic significance.

The fact is, throughout the history of the church there has been a great deal of diversity on the question of eschatology. Thus, through the centuries, faithful believers have differed greatly on the question of prophecy—and continue to do so.

Those that believe that prophecy is being fulfilled before our very eyes today, cite the transformation of Eastern Europe, the crisis in Iraq, the isolation of Israel, and the solidifying of the European Economic Community as specific signs that we are now living in the "Last Days." Wars and rumors of wars, famines, plagues, earthquakes, and pestilences—which all seem to be increasing in frequency and intensity—demonstrate beyond any shadow of a doubt that we have at last arrived at the "End Times."

In the Olivet Discourse—recorded in the Gospel of Matthew—Jesus attempts to calm such speculative fears. He tries to show that eschatological pessimism is not consistent with faith in His kingdom.

Following His prediction that the Temple in Jerusalem would soon be destroyed, His nervous disciples began to ask Him a series of questions:

> When will these things be? What will be the sign of Your coming? And what will be the sign of the end of this age? (Matthew 24:3)

Jesus responded by telling them that they had nothing to fear (Matthew 24:6). They were instead to be on guard against those who would unduly alarm and deceive them (Matthew 24:4). In spite of a spate of wars, rumors of wars, famines, pestilences, earthquakes, tribulation, and persecutions, they were to be assured that the end was not yet in sight (Matthew 24:6–12). In fact, He told them, these signs were just the beginnings of mankind's long and tortured struggle through history—the very birthpangs (Matthew 24:8).

Instead of focusing on these subjective and often misleading "Signs of the Times," Jesus directed their attention to the great task of preaching the gospel to all nations (Matthew 24:14).

Although His discourse is filled with specific portending prophecies—as the destruction of Jerusalem in 70 A.D. ultimately proved—the primary thrust of Christ's message was that eschatology is essentially ethical and only second-arily predictive. It is revealed by the good providence of God to provoke His people to uphold their responsibili-ties—to faithfully carry out the Great Commission, to dili-gently build up the church, to pray without ceasing, to en-gage in spiritual warfare, to serve the hurting and meet the needs of the innocent, to walk in holiness, and to live with one another in faith, hope, and love. In short, eschatology is a prod in the hands of God to incite the church to do right when all the rest of the world does wrong.

The New World Order is no match, after all, for the empowered people of Christ Jesus—for as scripture asserts "His dominion is an everlasting dominion which shall not pass away" (Daniel 4:34).

The Lessons of History

Kermit Roosevelt, the youngest son of Theodore Roosevelt, spent his life examining the problems of the Middle East. In 1949, he wrote very prophetically:

> Are we yet aware of the danger that in the Middle East the United Nations may come to be regarded and mis-trusted and hated as the guardian of the New World Order—the New Age trappings for the old Humanistic conspiracy of Left and Right together? The danger of Russia and the United States is the *seen* danger, and a grave one it is. Seen, it must in time be settled by peace or war. The danger of Orient versus Occident—of Is-lamic culture versus Christian culture—seems as yet *un-seen*. That could be ruinous. We may well succumb to it from not seeing. We must not assume in the days ahead that the crisis in the Middle East can be solved through military alliances, political connivance, or strategic initia-tive. Beware of the politicians or the coalitions that pro-pose such a solution—they may be fairly regarded, whether from the Left or the Right as a part of the same old entrenched interests that have stood against the Christian faith and have fought for a mechanical imposi-

tion of the New Age or the New World Order since the time of the Fall.[5]

Clearly, the New World Order is not a solution to the crisis in the Middle East. Instead, it is part and parcel of the crisis. It is, in fact, at the root of the crisis—with its only antidote being the faithful propagation of truth.

CHAPTER EIGHT

A TALE OF TWO HOUSE-HOLDS: CLASHING WORLDVIEWS

The world is at this moment passing through one of those terrible periods of convulsion when the souls of men and of nations are tried as by fire. Woe to the man or to the nation that at such a time stands as once Laodicea stood; as the people of ancient Meroz stood, when they dared not come to the help of the Lord against the mighty. In such a crisis the moral weakling is the enemy of the right, the enemy of life, liberty, and the pursuit of happiness.

Theodore Roosevelt

The kings of the earth take their stand, and the rulers take counsel together against the Lord and against His anointed.

Psalm 2:2

American foreign policy around the world and in the Middle East during the twentieth century has been, for all intents and purposes, the tale of two households. During the first half of the century, it was guided by the principles and precepts of the Roosevelts of Sagamore Hill. During the second half, it was guided by the principles and precepts of the Roosevelts of Hyde Park. The difference between the two was profound and has left a lasting impress upon the world in which we live.

Theodore Roosevelt, the patriarch of the Sagamore Hill side of the family, was a remarkable man of unbounded energies and many careers. Before his fiftieth birthday he had served the Republican party as a New York State legislator, the under-secretary of the Navy, police commissioner for the city of New York, United States civil service commissioner, the governor of New York, vice-president under William McKinley, a colonel in the United States Army, and two terms as president of the United States. In addition, he had written nearly thirty books, run a cattle ranch in the Dakota territories, and conducted scientific expeditions on four continents. He was a brilliant man who read at least five books every week of his life. He was a physical man who enjoyed hunting, boxing, and wrestling. He was a spiritual man who took his faith very seriously and for years taught Sunday school in his Dutch Reformed church. And he was a family man who lovingly raised five children and enjoyed a lifelong romance with his wife.

His distant cousin, Franklin Roosevelt, was the patriarch of the Hyde Park side of the family. He too was a remarkable man. A Harvard-educated lawyer, he began his political career as a Democratic party reformer in the New York State Senate. His vigorous campaign on behalf of Woodrow Wilson—against his famous cousin—during the 1912 presidential elections earned him an appointment as the assistant secretary of the Navy. In 1920 he was the vice-presidential running mate on the losing Democratic ticket. Eight years later, after a crippling bout with polio, he was elected to the first of two terms as New York's governor. Finally, in 1932 he ran for the presidency against the Depression-plagued Herbert Hoover and won overwhelmingly. During his record four terms he directed the ambitious transformation of American government, guided the nation through World War II, and laid the foundations for the United Nations.

Neither Theodore nor Franklin were isolationists in their foreign policy formulations, at least not in the same sense that Charles Lindberg or Robert Taft were. Both believed that America should play a significant role in the international community of nations. Both believed that America was the fulcrum of the modern world—that American strength, ingenuity, and principles should be exported to the farthest ends of the earth.

Even so, their differences were very significant. Theodore was a nationalist. Franklin was an internationalist.

Theodore was a reformer who wanted to firmly and faithfully reestablish the Old World Order. Franklin was a revolutionary who wanted to boldly and unashamedly usher in a New World Order.

Theodore's motto was "walk softly and carry a big stick." Franklin's motto was "good neighbors live in solidarity."

Theodore spoke forcefully but led the world into a remarkable epoch of peace; he even won the Nobel Peace Prize in 1905. Like his mentor Woodrow Wilson, Franklin spoke of peace but led the world into the bloodiest confrontation in man's tortured history.

The difference between these two perspectives was fundamental and presuppositional. Whereas Franklin's expansive global vision was informed by an unhesitatingly humanistic worldview, Theodore's focused civic vision was informed by an uncompromising Christian worldview. In fact, while Franklin rejected the faith of his fathers early in life, Theodore stood foursquare on the legacy of Biblical orthodoxy. He often asserted that he was "proud of my Holland, Huguenot, and Covenanting ancestors, and proud that the blood of that stark Puritan divine Jonathan Edwards flows in the veins" of his children.

The practical outworking of these two models for American foreign policy was dramatic: Franklin's led to bureaucracy, insecurity, and inefficiency at home, and war, tyranny, and neo-imperialism abroad. Theodore's led to prosperity, sagacity, and safety at home, and peace, liberty, and cooperation abroad.

Of the two perspectives, Theodore's was by far the most desirable and by far the most Biblical—adhering as it did to the mandate passed down by the Old Testament prophet Micah.

The Micah Mandate

In 1917, when American troops were preparing to sail across the seas to take to the battlefields of France and Belgium in the First World War, the New York Bible Society asked Theodore to inscribe a message in the pocket New Testaments that each soldier would be given. The great man happily complied:

> The teaching of the New Testament is foreshadowed in Micah's verse: "What more doth the Lord require of thee than to *do justice,* and to *love mercy,* and to *walk humbly* with thy God." *Do justice;* and therefore fight valiantly against those that stand for the reign of Moloch and Beelzebub on this earth. *Love mercy;* treat your enemies well; succor the afflicted; treat every woman as if she were your sister; care for the little children; and be tender with the old and helpless. *Walk humbly;* you will do so if you study the life and teachings of the Savior, walking in His steps. And remember: the most perfect machinery of government will not keep us as a nation from destruction if there is not within us a soul. No abounding of material prosperity shall avail us if our spiritual senses atrophy. The foes of our own household will surely prevail against us unless there be in our people an inner life which finds its outward expression in a morality like unto that preached by the seers and prophets of God when the grandeur that was Greece and the glory that was Rome still lay in the future.[1]

Theodore understood only too well the essence of Biblical ethics as it applied to public policy. He understood that the security of men and nations depends on faithful adherence to Micah's threefold demonstration of discipleship: a strident commitment to the just application of law (see Romans 2:11–24; James 2:8–13), a practical concern for the unfortunate (see James 1:27; Philippians 2:4), and a reverent fear of almighty God (see Acts 10:34–35; Proverbs 1:7). He knew that even with the deployment of superior forces in superior numbers with superior armaments, the American armies would ultimately be defeated during the war if they took to the field bereft of these essential spiritual resources.

Theodore self-consciously integrated these three standards into his foreign policy framework, thus creating a paradigm well worth emulating.

The Standard of Justice

During his tenure in Washington with the Civil Service Commission, Theodore wrote a biography of Gouverneur Morris—the great merchant, lawyer, and planter from Pennsylvania who had drafted the final version of the Constitution. Theodore, like Morris, believed that in order for the American experiment in liberty to succeed, justice and righteousness had to be welded together as one in the hearts and minds of the citizenry. He was thus fond of quoting Morris's famous maxim on the subject:

> Liberty and justice simply cannot be had apart from the gracious influences of a righteous people. A righteous people simply cannot exist apart from the aspiration to liberty and justice. The Christian religion and its incumbent morality is tied to the cause of freedom with a Gordian knot; loose one from the other and both are sent asunder.[2]

Throughout the Bible the attributes of justice and righteousness are inextricably linked. In more than sixty different passages all across the wide span of the Old and New Testaments, God's Word makes it plain that to attempt to secure life, liberty, and the pursuit of happiness

apart from the clearly revealed ethical parameters of good-
ness, truth, purity, faithfulness, and holiness is utter folly.
On the other hand, a people that diligently seeks to do
righteousness will inevitably pursue justice as well. The two
simply go together. One cannot be had without the other.

Again and again the refrain sounds:

- This is what the Lord says: Maintain justice and do
  what is right, for my salvation is close at hand and my
  righteousness will soon be revealed. (Isaiah 56:1)

- The Lord loves righteousness and justice. (Psalm 33:5)

- Righteousness and justice are the foundation of the
  Lord's throne. Love and faithfulness go before Him.
  (Psalm 89:14)

- In faithfulness He will bring forth justice. (Isaiah 42:3)

- He says: I will make justice the measuring line and
  righteousness the plumb line. (Isaiah 28:17)

- Blessed are they who maintain justice, who constantly
  do what is right. (Psalm 106:3)

- Learn to do right. Seek justice. (Isaiah 1:17)

- Hate evil, love good, and maintain justice. Perhaps the
  Lord God Almighty will have mercy. (Amos 5:15)

- Therefore, let justice roll on like a river, righteousness
  like a never-failing stream. (Amos 5:24)

Because Jesus emphasized this very unity between
moral purity and judicial integrity in His earthly ministry,
He continually found Himself in conflict with both the religious leaders and the secularists of His day. Neither cared
for His Biblically rooted insistence that justice was impossible apart from righteousness, and vice versa.

Theodore recognized and reasserted this connection
between justice and righteousness. He not only stood steadfast against the secular tendency to remove morality from
the arena of justice; he was equally vigilant in opposing the

religious tendency to remove justice from the arena of spirituality.

The Standard of Mercy

During his campaign speeches in 1912, Theodore often liked to quote the great American journalist, pastor, and statesman during the founding era, Morgan Fraser, who said:

> No tyrant can ere long rule a gracious and merciful people. Charity sows seeds of freedom that may not be suppressed, for charity naturally disposes authority to the charitable, and the charitable are naturally disposed to freedom. Thus, when the people of the Living God undertake the holy duty of caring for the needy, the poor, the brokenhearted, and the deprived, the perverse subverters of morality, truth and liberty are certain to be exposed and deposed.[3]

To Theodore this summarized his own ambition for America: to become rich in authority by becoming rich in service—to become great by becoming good.

One of the most basic principles of the Christian worldview is simply that the ability to lead a society is earned, not inherited. And it is earned through faithful, compassionate, and merciful service. Whoever becomes the benefactor of the people will ultimately be able to wield authority with them (see Luke 22:25).

Jesus said, "Blessed are the merciful, for they shall receive mercy" (Matthew 5:7). That is why he lived his life as a servant (see Luke 22:27). He came to serve, not to be served (see Matthew 20:28). He came offering mercy at every turn (see Mark 5:19; Matthew 9:13).

Not surprisingly, He called His disciples to a similar life of selfless giving (see Luke 22:26). He called us to be servants (see Matthew 19:30). He said, "Whoever wishes to be chief among you, let him be your servant" (Matthew 20:27). He said, "Be merciful, just as your Father is merciful" (Luke 6:36). The attitude of all aspiring leaders "should be the same as Christ's, who, being in very nature God, did not consider equality with God something to be grasped, but made Himself nothing, taking the very nature of a servant" (Philippians 2:5–7).

Theodore Roosevelt believed, based on this Biblical principle, that our nation's activities abroad ought not be motivated by greed, avarice, pragmatism, tradition, or any other artificial standard. Instead, they ought to be motivated by what is right and good and true. That is the confident posture of the servant leader—neither promiscuously acquiescent nor pompously irascible.

The Standard of Humility

In the days before American involvement in World War I, when the crisis in the Middle East had once again taken the world's center stage, Theodore urged the nation and its leaders to recognize the full dimensions of the conflict:

> Prayer is our greatest weapon in these or any other times. Best we not send our boys across the sea to face the heathen hoards lest we have a nation at home one in prayer. If history teaches us nothing else, let us at least remember what the Byzantines learned, what the Crusaders learned, and what the French learned: you cannot face the dread terror of Islam in mere human strength. When the quietude of the desert has been stirred, let all Christian men and women turn to the sovereign Lord. Let all Christian men and women turn to Him in holy seasons of prayer.[4]

In calling on the American people to recognize the spiritual dimensions of the conflict in the Middle East, Roosevelt was merely reiterating the philosophy of his great hero, George Washington, who asserted:

> It is the first duty of all nations to acknowledge the providence of almighty God, to obey His will, to be grateful

for His benefits, and to humbly implore His protection and favor in holy fear.[5]

Again, Washington said:

Of all the dispositions and habits which lead to civil prosperity, a humble fear before the Almighty and a life of Christian morality are indispensable supports. In vain would that man claim the attribute of patriotism, who should labor to subvert these great pillars of human happiness, these firmest props of the duties of men and citizens. A volume could not trace all their connections with private and public felicity. Let it simply be stated that there is no security for property, for reputation, or for life, if the sense of religious obligation desert the oaths, which are the instruments of investigation in courts of true justice.[6]

Roosevelt and Washington both understood that the most realistic approach to an issue—to any issue—is always theocentric. In other words, it begins and ends with a recognition that the Lord is the Alpha and the Omega of the whole created order (see Revelation 1:8) and that He exercises His sovereign control over it at all times and in all places (see Psalm 115:3).

The Bible is prolific in its assertion of this truth:

- The fear of the Lord is the beginning of wisdom; a good understanding have all those who do His commandments. His praise endures forever. (Psalm 111:10)

- The fear of the Lord is the beginning of knowledge, but fools despise wisdom and instruction. (Proverbs 1:7)

- The fear of the Lord prolongs days, but the years of the wicked will be shortened. (Proverbs 10:27)

- In the fear of the Lord is strong confidence, and His children will have a place of refuge. The fear of the Lord is a fountain of life, to avoid the snares of death. (Proverbs 14:26–27)

- Better is a little with the fear of the Lord, than great treasure with trouble. (Proverbs 15:16)

- Clothe yourselves in humility toward one another, for God is opposed to the proud, but gives grace to the humble. Humble yourselves therefore, under the mighty hand of God, that He may lift you up in due time, casting all your anxiety upon Him because He cares for you. (1 Peter 5:5-7)

A nation whose leaders are humbled in fear before God will suffer no want (see Psalm 34:9). It will surely be blessed (see Psalm 115:13). And, it will be set high above all the nations of the earth (see Deuteronomy 28:1).

This is the fundamental truth that underlies the Christian worldview and the motivation that drove Theodore Roosevelt's approach to foreign policy in the Middle East.

Prophecy and the Cultural Mandate

There are doomsayers and there are naysayers. The doomsayers argue that the "End" is upon us, the "Last Days" have come, the sky is falling, and all is lost. The naysayers argue that there is nothing to worry about, everything is under control, things can only get better, and the "New Age" is nigh unto us.

Neither perspective is Biblical. And neither perspective is responsible.

After the Ascension of Christ, the disciples were awestruck—staring into the clouds. In short order though, two angelic messengers came and rebuked them:

Men of Galilee, why do you stand gazing up into heaven? (Acts 1:11)

Jesus had given them a job to do. But here they were paralyzed with wonder. Jesus had called them to evangelize the world. But here they were loitering in recalcitrance. Jesus had promised them power and unction. But here they were frozen in the grips of hysteria. Jesus had commanded them to "occupy" the earth until He returned. But here they were occupied only with their own wild speculations.

Sadly little has changed for many of Christ's disciples. They are still "looking steadfastly into the clouds" (Acts 1:9) instead of fulfilling their mandate to win the world with justice, mercy, and humility.

Theodore Roosevelt had little patience for either doomsayers or naysayers. He built a foreign policy on the notion that Christ meant what He had said. Can we do anything less?

The Lessons of History

In January 1776, George Wythe of Virginia asked John Adams to draw up a plan that would enable the American colonies to establish a constitutional system strong enough to survive the rigors of war with England and to meet the challenges of the months and years that followed. Adams replied with his usual discernment, discretion, and wisdom.

> The foundation of every nation is some principle or passion in the minds of the people. The noblest principles and most generous affections in our Christian character, then, have the fairest chance to support the noblest and the most generous models of civil covenant. If liberty and justice for all men is to be ensured then we cannot, we dare not, we must not stray from the Writ of right.[7]

Indeed, ideas have consequences. Worldviews make a difference. Covenants alter the course of cultures and ultimately of all of history. To fail to realize this basic and fundamental truth is to miss the import of social relations in this poor fallen world altogether.

CHAPTER NINE

THE DAWNING OF THE DAY: POSTLUDE TO WAR

We belong to quite as many regiments as the German Kaiser. Our regiments are regiments that are embattled everywhere; they fight an unending fight against all that is hopeless and rapacious and of evil report. The only difference is that we have the regiments, but not the uniforms.

G.K. Chesterton

If my people who are called by My Name will humble themselves, and pray, and seek My face, and turn from their wicked ways, then I will hear from heaven, and will forgive their sin, and heal their land.

2 Chronicles 7:14

The sun rose over the Kidron Valley in deep shades of scarlet. From my hotel window I could see the Old City begin to come to life, its austere enchantment scarred and fluted with the trampled paths of the aeons.

Below me I saw a small cluster of tourists—an all too uncommon sight in these dire days. They began to walk toward the Jaffa Gate very slowly, as if savoring every precious morsel of time and space. An air of sanctity clothed them. They seemed hushed by awe. It is deep in man to love the place where Divinity has walked. To pray here. To tread these streets and to touch these stones. It offers us a momentary communion. And so the holy sites multiply under our fervor, however tenuous their roots in history.

A few blocks from where the tourists walked, a quiet procession made its way toward the entrance to the Church of the Holy Sepulcher. Monks with long gnarled beards and cloaked in fraying robes held their tapers before them, cherishing their heritage as a fountain in the emptiness. The sweet fragrance of their censers and the haunting refrains of their chants anointing.

Still deeper into the city, beyond the ancient battlements of Suleiman, the *Hasidim* were gathering for prayer at the Western Wall. They were clearly people in the ebbtide of tradition. A few of the men wore startling robes of fawn, belted at the waist like dressing gowns, but most of them were veiled entirely in dusty black—thin, long coats and wide, perched hats. Their unbarbered beards gushed in all directions. Their sun-gingered ringlets either curled round their ears or dangled like gilt-cords in the sanctuary. Their faces were gaunt with the tautness of the ghetto. With their prayer shawls unfurled, they cried out to Jehovah both together and separately—the irony of which is the essence of the Judaic community and its worship.

And above them, on the wraith of Herod's Temple— the paved loneliness of a mountain plateau—a ragged line of the *Umma* walked silently into the shrine of Mohammed's mysterious transport. Under its vast, empty dome, the pious souls went through their actions carefully. They stood, they touched their foreheads to the ground in prayer, they clasped their hands on their stomachs, and they patted their knees. There was nothing self-conscious in their gestures. Their humility was genuine—expressed in a formal and dignified service unchanged by the passing of centuries.

I saw all this from the vantage of my window and was struck with wonder. Deep within I heard an echo of the ancient cantor's plea:

Jerusalem is built as a city that is compact together, where all the tribes go up, even the tribes of the Lord, to the testimony of the Covenant, to give thanks to the Name of the Lord. Therefore thrones are set there for judgment, even the thrones of the House of David. Pray for the peace of Jerusalem. (Psalm 122:3–6, NKJV)

But as I turned from the casement, I realized that the peace of Jerusalem would never—and could never—be realized out of the cacophony of either human ambition or devotion. It would not—and could not—be achieved by the disparate souls below me. Waging peace is always a more treacherous affair than waging war. If fact, it can only be realized by fealty to Christ:

Why do the nations rage, and the people plot a vain thing? The kings of the earth set themselves, and rulers take counsel together, against the LORD and against His Anointed, saying, "Let us break Their bonds in pieces and cast away Their cords from us." He who sits in the Heavens shall laugh; the LORD shall hold them in derision. Then He shall speak to them in His wrath, and distress them in His deep displeasure: "Yet I have set My King on My holy hill of Zion." "I will declare the decree: The LORD has said to Me, 'You are My Son, today I have begotten You. Ask of Me, and I will give You the nations for Your inheritance, and the ends to the earth for Your possession. You shall break them with a rod of iron; You shall dash them to pieces like a potter's vessel.'" Now therefore, be wise, O kings; be instructed, you judges of the earth. Serve the LORD with fear, and rejoice with trembling. Kiss the Son, lest He be angry, and you perish in the way, when His wrath is kindled but a little. Blessed are all those who put their trust in Him. (Psalm 2:1–12, NKJV)

NOTES

Acknowledgements

1. Theodore Roosevelt, *Foes of Our Own Household* (New York: Charles Scribner's Sons, 1917), 137.

Introduction

1. Charles Haddon Spurgeon, *John Ploughman's Pictures* (Philadelphia: John Altemus), 137.
2. Ibid.

Chapter One: As the Moon Rises and Sets: Prelude to War

1. Quoted in *The New York Times,* August 7, 1990.
2. *Newsweek,* July 6, 1970.
3. Ibid.
4. *Church History,* 9:1, February 1990.

Chapter Three: The Sons of Ham: Ancient Empires and Recurring Dreams

1. Quoted in Al Hurriya, *From Nebuchadnezzar to Saddam Hussein: Babylon Rises Again,* fourth edition (Baghdad: Iraqi Ministry of Information and Culture, 1987, 1990), 7.
2. Ibid., 9.
3. Quoted in *Ha Ubal Or,* Jerusalem edition, January 3, 1991.
4. Ibid.
5. Quoted in James L. Baehr, *Leadership in the East: An Examination of the Passing Patriarchal Order* (Boston: Society of Political Science University Studies, 1973), 127–128.
6. Quoted in *Al Watan Kuwait,* October 4, 1981.
7. Ibid.
8. Quoted in Thomas W. Lippman, *Understanding Islam* (New York: New American Library, 1982), 116.
9. Ibid., 117.
10. Ibid.
11. Ibid.

Chapter Four: East of His Brothers: Ishmael and Isaac

1. Quoted in *The Middle East Business Report,* November, 1990.
2. Quoted in *Ha Ubal Or,* Jerusalem edition, January 3, 1991.
3. Ibid.
4. Quoted in Louis R. Essher, *Exile and Exodus: The Jewish-British Regiments in World War II* (London: Jackson-Poore, Ltd., 1961), 84.
5. Quoted in *New Dimensions Magazine,* January, 1991.
6. Ibid.
7. Quoted in *Ha Ubal Or,* Jerusalem edition, January 3, 1991.
8. Ibid.
9. Quoted in *Jerusalem Post,* December 14, 1990.
10. Ibid.
11. Quoted in *The PLO: Has It Complied with Its Commitments?* (Israel: Ministry of Foreign Affairs, August, 1990), 20.
12. Quoted in *Al Qabas Kuwait,* December 19, 1989.

Chapter Five: Ji'had: The Unending War of Conquest

1. Quoted in *The Glory of Byzantine Rome* (Zagreb, Croatia: Orthodox International Press, 1979), 37.
2. Ibid., 39.
3. Ibid., 62.
4. Quoted in *Al Sha'ab Cairo,* July, 1982.
5. Quoted in Tim Dowley, ed. *Lion Handbook to the History of Christianity* (Oxford: Lion Publishing Plc., 1977, 1990), 227.
6. Ibid.
7. Quoted in *The Dhimmi Newsletter,* October 1990.
8. Iman Khomeini, *Excerpts from Speeches and Messages of Iman Khomeini on the Unity of Moslems* (Tehran: Ministry of Islamic Guidance, 1979), 2.
9. Ibid., 4.
10. Ibid., 5.
11. Ibid., 4.
12. Quoted in Lester Mayfield-Owen, *Foxholes, Faith, and the First World War* (Phoenix, AZ: Liberty Bell Publishing House, 1971), 97.

Chapter Six: Loose Ends: The Peace to End All Peace

1. Quoted in Martin Forbes, *History Lessons: The Importance of Cultural Memory (New York: Palamir Publications, 1981), 112.*
2. Ibid., 113.
3. G. K. Chesterton, *Orthodoxy* (Garden City, NY: Image Books, 1959), 81.

Chapter Seven: Back to Babel: The New World Order

1. Quoted in *The McAlvany Intelligence Advisor,* October 1990.
2. Quoted in Michael H. Larour, *The Inklings and Their Influences* (London: S. F. G. & L. Presentations, 1986), 9.
3. Paul Johnson, *Modern Times: The World from the Twenties to the Eighties* (New York: Harper & Row, 1983), 689.
4. Quoted in *The McAlvany Intelligence Advisor,* October 1990.
5. Quoted in David L. Johnson, *Theodore Roosevelt: American Monarch* (Philadelphia: American History Sources, 1981), 191.

Chapter Eight: A Tale of Two Households: Clashing Worldviews

1. Theodore Roosevelt, *Foes of Our Household* (New York: Charles Scribner's Sons, 1917), 3.
2. James Carter Braxton, *Gouverneur Morris: A Biographical Sketch* (Charleston, SC: Braden-Lowell Press, 1911), 99.
3. Morgan Fraser, *Sermons, Discourses, and Essays* (New York: Braun and Cie, 1921), 63.
4. Quoted in David L. Johnson, *Theodore Roosevelt: American Monarch* (Philadelphia: American History Sources, 1981), 193.
5. Evan Davis, *Our Greatest President* (New York: Bedford Company, Publishers, 1891), 361.
6. Ibid., 366.
7. Quoted in Lamar P. Poirot, *The Adams Family: Four Generations of Service* (Quincy, MA: Truther and Forbes, Publishers, 1921), 109.

BIBLIOGRAPHIC RESOURCES

Bakhash, Shaul. *The Reign of the Ayatollahs: Iran and the Islamic Revolution*. New York: Basic Books, 1984, 1986.

Belloc, Hilaire. *The Jews*. London: Butler and Tanner, 1922.

Bill, James A., and Leiden, Carl. *The Middle East: Politics and Power*. Boston: Allyn and Bacon, 1974.

Bolitho, William. *Twelve Against the Gods: The Story of Adventure*. New York: The Readers Club, 1941.

Burton, Sir Richard F. *The Jew, The Gypsy and El Islam*. Allen and Davies, 1898.

Chilton, David. *Paradise Restored: A Biblical Eschatology of Victory*. Fort Worth, TX: Dominion Press, 1985.

Collins, Larry, and Lapierre, Dominique. *O Jerusalem!* London: Grafton Books, 1982.

Cook, Michael. *Muhammad*. New York: Oxford University Press, 1983.

Darsh, Dr. S. M. *Muslims In Europe*. London: Ta-Ha Publishers, 1980.

de Camp, L. Sprague. *The Ancient Engineers*. New York: Ballantine, 1963.

de Villiers, Gerard; Touchais, Bernard; and de Villiers, Annick V. *The Imperial Shah: An Informal Biography*. Boston: Little, Brown and Co., 1976.

Deacon, Richard. *The Israeli Secret Service*. New York: Sphere Books, 1979.

Durant, Will. *Our Oriental Heritage. The Story of Civilization,* vol. 1. New York: Simon and Schuster, 1954.

Dyer, Charles. *The Rise of Babylon.* Wheaton, IL: Tyndale House Publications, 1991.

Fischer, Michael M. J. *Iran: From Religious Dispute to Revolution.* Cambridge, MA: Harvard University Press, 1980.

Follett, Ken. *On Wings of Eagles.* New York: Signet, 1983.

Friedman, Thomas L. *From Beirut to Jerusalem.* New York: Anchor Books, 1989.

Fromkin, David. *A Peace to End All Peace: The Fall of the Ottoman Empire and the Creation of the Modern Middle East.* New York: Avon Books, 1989.

Goode, Stephen. *The Prophet and the Revolutionary: Arab Socialism and the Modern Middle East.* New York: Franklin Watts, 1975.

Hamada, Louis Bahjat. *Understanding the Arab World.* Nashville, TN: Thomas Nelson Publishers, 1990.

Hamilton, Rita. *The Poem of the Cid.* Translated by Janet Perry. New York: Penguin Books, 1985.

Herzl, Theodor. *The Jewish State.* New York: Dover Publications, 1946.

Herzog, Chaim. *The Arab-Israeli Wars: War and Peace in the Middle East from the War of Independence Through Lebanon.* New York: Vintage Books, 1984.

Hinnells, John R., ed. *A Handbook of Living Religions.* New York: Pelican Books, 1985.

Holt, P. M., Lambton, Anne K. S., and Lewis, Bernard, eds. *The Cambridge History of Islam,* vol. 1A. New York: Cambridge University Press, 1970.

Holt, P. M., Lambton, Anne K. S., and Lewis, Bernard, eds. *The Cambridge History of Islam,* vol. 1B. New York: Cambridge University Press, 1970.

Holt, P. M., Lambton, Anne K. S., and Lewis, Bernard, eds. *The Cambridge History of Islam,* vol. 2A. New York: Cambridge University Press, 1970.

Ibraham, Ishak. *Black Gold and Holy War.* Nashville, TN: Thomas Nelson, 1983.

Johnson, Paul. *A History of the Jews.* New York: Harper and Row, 1987.

Jordan, James B. *The Bible and the Nations.* Tyler, TX: Biblical Horizons, 1988.

Kapuscinski, Ryszard. *Shah of Shahs.* New York: Vintage Books, 1982.

Khalil, Samir al. *Republic of Fear: The Inside Story of Saddam's Iraq.* New York: Pantheon, 1989.

Kinross, Lord. *The Ottoman Centuries: The Rise and Fall of the Turkish Empire.* New York: Marrow Quill, 1977.

Kritzeck, James, ed. *Anthology of Islamic Literature: From the Rise of Islam to Modern Times.* New York: New American Library, 1964.

Lamb, David. *The Arabs: Journeys Beyond the Mirage.* New York: Vintage Books, 1987.

Lancaster, Pat, ed. *Traveller's Guide to the Middle East.* Edison, NJ: Hunter Publishing, 1988.

Lapidus, Ira M. *A History of Islamic Societies.* New York: Cambridge University Press, 1988.

Lippman, Thomas. *Understanding Islam: An Introduction to the Moslem World.* New York: Mentor, 1982.

Loffreda, Stanislao. *Recovering Capharnaum.* Italy: Poligrafico Artioli-Modena, 1985.

Lunt, James. *Hussein of Jordan.* London: Fontana, 1990.

Mace, John. *Modern Persian.* New York: Hodder and Stoughton, 1962.

Macfie, A. L. *The Eastern Question 1774–1923.* New York: Longman, 1989.

McDowell, Josh, and Gilchrist, John. *The Islam Debate.* San Bernardino, CA: Here's Life, 1983.

McKinnon, Dan. *Bullseye Iraq.* New York: Berkeley Books, 1988.

Miller, Judith, and Mylroie, Laurie. *Saddam Hussein and the Crisis in the Gulf.* New York: Times Books, 1990.

The Ministry of Foreign Affairs. *The PLO: Has It Complied with Its Commitments—Update August '90.* Jerusalem: Israel Information Center, 1990.

Mortimer, Edward. *Faith and Power: The Politics of Islam.* New York: Vintage Books, 1982.

Naipaul, V. S. *Among the Believers: An Islamic Journey.* New York: Vintage Books, 1981.

Newell, Richard S., and Newell, Nancy Peabody. *The Struggle for Afghanistan.* Ithaca, NY: Cornell University Press, 1981.

North, Gary. *Healer of the Nations: Biblical Blueprints for International Relations.* Biblical Blueprints Series, vol. 9. Fort Worth, TX: Dominion Press, 1987.

Payne, Robert. *The Dream and the Tomb: A History of the Crusades.* New York: Stein and Day, 1984.

Pierce, Rev. James Wilson. *Story of Turkey and Armenia.* Baltimore: R. H. Woodward Co., 1896.

Pryce-Jones, David. *The Closed Circle: An Interpretation of the Arabs.* London: Paladin, 1990.

Reed, Douglas. *The Controversy of Zion.* Durban, Natal, South Africa: Dolphin Press, 1978.

Riley-Smith, Jonathan. *The Crusades: A Short History.* New Haven: Yale University Press, 1987.

Rivers, Gayle. *The War Against the Terrorists: How to Win It.* New York: Stein and Day, 1986.

Rivers, Gayle, and Hudson, James. *The Teheran Contract.* New York: Bantam Books, 1982.

Roosevelt, Kermit. *Countercoup: The Struggle for the Control of Iran.* New York: McGraw-Hill, 1979.

Rubin, Barry. *Paved With Good Intentions: The American Experience and Iran.* New York: Penguin Books, 1982.

Runciman, Steven. *The Fall of Constantinople 1453.* New York: Cambridge University Press, 1965.

Runciman, Steven. *The First Crusade and the Foundations of the Kingdom of Jerusalem.* A History of the Crusades, vol. 1. New York: Cambridge University Press, 1951.

Runciman, Steven. *The Kingdom of Jerusalem and the Frankish East 1100—1187.* A History of the Crusades, vol. 2. New York: Cambridge University Press, 1952.

Runciman, Steven. *The Kingdom of Acre and the Later Crusades.* A History of the Crusades, vol. 3. New York: Cambridge University Press, 1954.

Runciman, Steven. *The Great Church in Captivity: A Study of the Patriarchite of Constantinople from the Eve of the Turkish Conquest to the Greek War of Independence.* New York: Cambridge University Press, 1968.

Ryan, Paul B. *The Iranian Rescue Mission: Why It Failed.* Annapolis, MD: Naval Institute Press, 1985.

Saikal, Amin. *The Rise and Fall of the Shah.* Princeton, NJ: Princeton University Press, 1980.

Sanders, N. K. *The Epic of Gilgamesh.* New York: Penguin Books, 1960.

Sayers, Dorothy L. trans. *The Song of Roland.* New York: Penguin Books, 1957.

Sick, Gary. *All Fall Down: America's Tragic Encounter with Iran.* New York: Random House, 1985.

Simpson, John. *Behind Iranian Lines: Travels Through Revolutionary Iran and the Persian Past.* London: Fontana, 1989.

Sivan, Emmanuel. *Radical Islam: Medieval Theology and Modern Politics*. New Haven: Yale University Press, 1990.

Stark, Freya. *The Journey's Echo*. New York: The Ecco Press, 1988.

Taheri, Amir. *The Spirit of Allah: Khomeini and the Islamic Revolution*. Bethesda, MD: Adler and Adler, 1986.

Theroux, Peter. *Sandstorms: Days and Nights in Arabia*. New York: Norton, 1990.

Tritton, A. S. *Islam: Belief and Practices*. New York: Hutchinson's University Library, 1951.

Tuchman, Barbara. *Bible and Sword: England and Palestine from the Bronze Age to Balfour*. New York: Ballantine, 1984.

Twain, Mark. *The Innocents Abroad*. New York: Signet, 1980.

Wallach, John and Janet. *Still Small Voices*. New York: Citadel Press, 1990.

Wheeler, Tony. *West Asia on a Shoestring*. Berkeley, CA: Lonely Planet, 1990.

Widlanski, Michael. *Can Israel Survive a Palestinian State?* Jerusalem: Institute for Advanced Strategic and Political Studies, 1990.

Zaehner, R. C. *Hindu and Muslim Mysticism*. New York: Schocken Books, 1969.

Zakaria, Rafiq. *The Struggle Within Islam: The Conflict Between Religion and Politics*. New York: Penguin, 1988.

ıno€x

131

ABOUT THE AUTHOR

George Grant is a popular speaker and a prolific author. His books include *Bringing in the Sheaves: Transforming Poverty into Productivity, Trial and Error: The American Civil Liberties Union and Its Impact on Your Family, Third Time Around: The History of the Pro-Life Movement from the First Century to the Present,* and the award winning exposé of the abortion industry, *Grand Illusions: The Legacy of Planned Parenthood.* His academic studies in political science were conducted at the University of Houston.

Mr. Grant is the executive director of Coral Ridge Ministries in Fort Lauderdale, Florida, where he lives with his wife and three children. He is currently at work on a novel and a series of biographies.

The typeface for the text of this book is *Baskerville*. Its creator, John Baskerville (1706-1775), broke with tradition to reflect in his type the rounder, yet more sharply cut lettering of eighteenth-century stone inscriptions and copy books. The type foreshadows modern design in such novel characteristics as the increase in contrast between thick and thin strokes and the shifting of stress from the diagonal to the vertical strokes. Realizing that this new style of letter would be most effective if cleanly printed on smooth paper with genuinely black ink, he built his own presses, developed a method of hot pressing the printed sheet to a smooth, glossy finish, and experimented with special inks. However, Baskerville did not enter into general commercial use in England until 1923.

Substantive Editing:
Michael S. Hyatt

Copy Editing:
Peggy Moon

Cover Design:
Steve Diggs & Friends
Nashville, Tennessee

Page Composition:
Xerox Ventura Publisher
Printware 720 IQ Laser Printer

Printing and Binding:
Maple-Vail Book Manufacturing Group
York, Pennsylvania

Cover Printing:
Strine Printing Company
York, Pennsylvania